COMMONSENSE
MARKETING
for
NON-MARKETERS

COMMONSENSE
MARKETING
for
NON-MARKETERS

Straightforward techniques
for spectacular results!

ALISON BAVERSTOCK

Foreword by STUART SMITH, Editor *Marketing Week*

PIATKUS

Copyright © 1995 Alison Baverstock
Foreword Copyright © 1995 Stuart Smith

First published in Great Britain in 1995 by
Judy Piatkus (Publishers) Ltd of
5 Windmill Street, London W1P 1HF

First paperback edition 1997

The moral right of the author has been asserted

*A catalogue record for this book is available
from the British Library*

ISBN 0–7499–1627–3

Typeset by Action Typesetting Limited, Gloucester
Printed and bound in Great Britain by
Biddles Ltd, Guildford and King's Lynn

Contents

Acknowledgements

There are many people I would like to thank for reading sections of my book and making comments. In particular I would like to thank Jamie Pennington who read the entire manuscript during his summer holiday, not once but twice, and George Riddiford of Brewer Riddiford whom I consulted during the early stages of my research and referred back to at regular intervals. Thanks also to Stuart Smith, Editor of *Marketing Week*, for writing the foreword.

I would also like to thank: David Archibald; David Ogilvy; Paul Chadwick of Arthur Young Associates; John Carter, Management Consultant; David Lowings of Dragon International; Judith Meddick; Mary Hammond of Kodak Corporate Communications; Nicola Potts of the Market Research Association; Leslie Henry of Book Marketing Ltd; Philip Spink and Mike Waterson of the Advertising Association; Chris Rowat of the Institute of Logistics; Desmond Clarke of ITPS; Norman Melvin of Gallup; Vivienne Pringle of Blooming Marvellous; Andrew Welham of Penguin Books; Alina Lourie of Macmillan; Jeanette Hull of the Direct Mail Information Service; George Goodwin, Public Relations Specialist; Fiona Brownlee of Pavilion; David Rees of Penyards; Jane Barlow of the *Folkestone Extra*, Brian McDill of Wincanton Distribution Ltd; Nicola Price of Verdict Research Ltd.

For the kind permission to reproduce samples of their advertisements, I would like to thank the Advertising Standards Authority, CCA Galleries, Lands' End Direct Merchants UK Ltd and the Michigan Information Centre. Thanks also to Christine King of British Telecommunications plc for permission to reproduce a BT press release.

Finally thanks to Neil for controlling the computer, reading the manuscript and encouragement throughout, and to Hamish for the deadline.

Foreword

Anita Roddick once asked *Marketing Week* to explain marketing to her. She was about to speak at the Marketing Society and felt that she needed an authoritative definition.

Of course, we needn't take this false modesty too seriously. If Roddick, founder of the Body Shop, doesn't know what marketing is about, no one does. But it's a pretty reasonable bet that neither she nor that other great intuitive marketer, Richard Branson, has ever studied a marketing textbook in their life. However, most non-professional marketers, baffled by the thicket of MBA jargon which unnecessarily surrounds the subject, need a little more assistance. They will find plenty of it in *Commonsense Marketing for Non-Marketers*, which is written in jargon-free, intelligible English.

Marketing is not a science, although there are plenty of people who would like to convince you that it is. Marketing is a skill which anyone can acquire. It is about selling goods and services to consumers who want them, at a reasonable price, while making a long-term profit for the manufacturer or provider.

Besides providing a clear understanding of the working principles of marketing, *Commonsense Marketing for Non-Marketers* tackles some widespread misconceptions about the subject. People often conclude that marketing is wasteful, frivolous or even pernicious, when they see expensive advertising campaigns on the television and mountains of mailshots on their doormat. They are reluctant to accept that they are affected by marketing (specifically advertising, the most visible weapon in the marketing armoury) and yet are at the same time deeply suspicious of its 'manipulative' and 'intrusive' nature.

These misconceptions arise from judging the marketing activity itself in isolation from the aims which drive it. Quite simply, if marketing initiatives did not create long-term sales and profit, they would not exist. The best marketing campaigns work not through manipulation (admen are not that clever or powerful), but by persuasion. A quick sale is of no use to a company if the customer is disappointed in the product or service and subsequently rejects the brand that is being promoted.

Good marketing improves availability and brings prices down by creating mass demand for products and services. Marketing is not some kind of cost-penalty passed on to the consumer in the form of higher prices.

In today's fickle, fast-moving world, those who become proficient in marketing can stay one step ahead of their competitors; those who do not are an endangered species.

Stuart Smith – Editor, *Marketing Week*
London, July 1995

Introduction

There are literally thousands of books on marketing. None of them is quite like this one.

This is deliberate. [Marketing today means different things to different people. On the one hand it has entered our day-to-day vocabulary – we talk about companies carrying out marketing campaigns and marketing surveys. On the other hand, marketing has become the subject of increasing academic debate. But no one, not even the academics, seems to know precisely what it means.)

What does seem to be true is that we are all a little wary of marketing. There is a general acceptance that marketing involves selling (although the American phrase 'going marketing', instead of 'going shopping', has not caught on here as yet). The British public don't regard selling with any great respect; they live in constant fear of being sold something they don't want, and being 'conned' in the process. At the same time, big marketing campaigns make good copy for journalists who love to feature stories of expensive promotions that have wasted lots of money.

For example, a well-publicised half-million-pound payout for a redesign of British Telecom's logo was widely seen as a waste of money. (To add insult to injury, the new logo had to be printed in two colours, making all BT's subsequent printing more expensive.) Similarly, chain stores in the run-up to Christmas, or banks looking for new customers, have spent fortunes on expensive television and press advertising, only to find their campaigns falling flat on their faces because the actual service could not live up to the claims made.

Meanwhile the academic study of marketing, with its continual creation of new jargon, makes us all feel like outsiders. A friend of mine completed an MBA eighteen months ago and tells me that even in that short time the marketing lingo has changed.

This jargon is probably most obvious in the trade press, where 'marketing speak' can make even the simplest concepts sound extremely complicated. Job advertisements are a very good example of this. A position on offer is a 'unique' opportunity for individuals not simply to work, but to demonstrate their 'handling capacity' as they 'lead the function'. Potential applicants must offer 'integrated and strategic creativity' in the pursuit of 'solutions' in the environment/situation', often for a 'profit responsible marketing role'. Each must obtain the necessary experience to 'differentiate an application' from other candidates who too have spent time showing that they have 'proven achievement in a competitive environment' and can 'add commercial value' to whatever they touch, preferably by an ability to 'maximise our brand proposition'. Above all, each must be a 'team-leader', offering 'strategy and support', all the while showing that 'effective team-work with functional colleagues is paramount'. Applicants are also, of course, utterly 'professional and committed'. Committed? After reading that lot you'll probably wish you could be.

Hence the need for this book, which offers a completely jargon-free approach to the subject. It will explain what marketing is, how it works (a set of principles that can be considered *whatever* you are promoting), what services are available and how to do it yourself. It will help all those buying marketing services – whether out-house from suppliers or in-house from their colleagues – to get *better value for money*.

1

What Marketing Means

You've probably noticed that most books on marketing start with an attempt to define what marketing is. So does mine.

I am not going to apologise for starting an unconventional book on marketing in such a conventional way; marketing today has become a pseudo-science. There is so much jargon being used that no one is entirely sure what anybody else is talking about. It's very important to set some ground rules.

What are the basics of marketing?

Professor Michael J. Baker of the Department of Marketing at Strathclyde University (see Further Reading) breaks marketing down into four essential components:

1 Start with the customer.

2 Take a long perspective.

3 Make full use of all the company's resources.

4 Innovate and be flexible.

This is a very useful structure and I will start by examining each of these elements in further detail, and then add two more of my own:

5 Marketing depends on relationships.

6 Marketing is a logical process.

1   Start with the customer

Although marketing professionals love to debate the meaning of marketing, they all share one central belief: the customer is of crucial importance. This is the major theme of every definition of marketing:

> 'Marketing is the performance of a business's activities that directs the flow of goods and services from producer to *consumer or user.*'
>
> AMERICAN MARKETING ASSOCIATION

> 'There is only one valid definition of business purpose: to create a *customer.*'
>
> PETER DRUCKER
> (*See Further Reading.*)

> 'Marketing is the whole business seen from the point of view of its final result, that is from the *customer's* point of view.'
>
> PETER DRUCKER

> 'Marketing means finding out what people want and giving it to them.'
>
> MALCOLM H.B. McDONALD
> (*See Further Reading.*)

Marketing depends on what people outside the organisation think, want and need. The aim of marketing is to define and satisfy the customer's needs better. This is achieved by trying to create an exchange that satisfies all parties; juggling different factors, such as production and distribution, but all the while keeping the customer in the centre.

Judith Meddick put this more simply: 'Marketing means looking at your organisation from the outside.'

This means dropping your own inside knowledge and undoubted preference for your own products and thinking about your company as the *customer* sees it. Demand for any product depends on how the potential customer views it: do they have the need, the means and the will to purchase? In a nutshell: 'No customers, no business'.

Following on from this, there is a vital distinction between being *market led* rather than *production led*; the determination to *make what you can sell* rather than trying to *sell what you can make*.

Market led companies put the needs of the customer first, and then think about what they can make to meet them. Production-orientated companies take 'what we can make' as their starting point and then think about whom it can be sold to. Consequently, this reduces the chance of totally satisfying the customer.

2   Take a long perspective

Marketing depends on long-term relationships. You are unlikely to understand what motivates a market straight away, unless you already possess a long-term understanding of your customers' needs and priorities. Establishing or enlarging a marketing department, or suddenly increasing the marketing budget, will not instantly produce good marketing.

Good marketing must involve long-term strategy and planning: keeping up to date with social, political and economic trends in order to understand which way the market is moving. This feedback can be used to refine the product range over the longer term: perhaps preparing different versions of a product for different markets; identifying or even creating new market trends; drafting contingency plans.

All this information provides the basis for a long-term plan, to be continuously updated. If the long-term goals are clear, the organisation is free to respond quickly and imaginatively to short-term opportunities and threats as they arise. And management goals clearly explained to the workforce will motivate the rest of the staff to want to get there too.

Finally, only with long-term planning can you truly be rooted in reality. You can't predict the future, but taking a long-term view will give you a much better chance of distinguishing between underlying trends and temporary blips; between hype (whether created or fostered by you) and genuine trends.

Internet.

3   Make full use of all the company's resources

To work successfully, marketing has to be part of the fundamental structure of a business. This does not mean it has to be the largest part of the organisation – indeed, if marketing goals are fully adopted, a specific 'marketing department' may not be needed at all.

Properly managed, marketing should be a complex coordination of all the different factors which constitute the company, its operations and its future. As Colin McIver (see Further Reading) put it:

> Marketing is not a self-contained discipline that produces results in isolation from other managerial functions, such as production, purchasing, personnel and finance. It's a vital management function that needs to be skilfully blended with all the other functions that add up to a successful business.

4   Innovate and be flexible

A full understanding of markets leads to innovation; because if customers' needs are not being met completely, there are potential markets for better versions of existing products as well as new products or services.

Most of marketing's big successes now look to have been obvious gaps in the market; they are new goods for existing or new markets. But whilst they may *look* obvious now, they are by definition hard to predict. (If they had looked obvious at the time they would have been obvious to everyone.) For example, the Body Shop struck a real chord because British society in the early 1980s agreed it wanted cosmetics with less packaging and hype and more environmental friendliness. Other household names too have come into existence relatively recently offering innovative versions of existing services. Toys R Us and McDonalds only started selling franchises in 1955; Rank Xerox shares first became available in 1958.

As well as the need to be innovative, there is a need for flexibility as market conditions change. Customers are not constant. Most products have a similar life cycle: after a slow initial uptake, when a product first goes on sale, if all goes well there is a consumer-rush. But you cannot rely on this rush for ever. Competitors will come along with 'me too' products, usually at a cheaper price, and the market will become saturated. A consumer's basic loyalty is to his or her own interests and change is inevitable.

Market-orientated companies are flexible; they adapt as market conditions change. Ideally, they anticipate the way the market is moving and change just before. Companies that stick to a narrow product base and, as markets decline, concentrate their efforts solely on searching for new markets for their range, are likely to die.

5 Marketing depends on relationships

According to P. Kotler, one of the best-known marketing theoreticians, marketing is: 'A social and managerial process by which individuals and groups obtain what they need and want through creating and exchanging products and value with others.'

There is one crucial element worth emphasising here which we will return to. *Marketing is not something that can be carried on in isolation; it depends on relationships.* Even the most basic subsistence economies depend on relationships between traders who communicate to barter goods in return for staple crops. The same principle holds good for today's multinational companies: if you ignore relationships with staff, with customers, shareholders or even potential

employees your chances of success will be severely compro-
mised. Marketing is a social process.

6   Marketing is a logical process

The public image of marketing is often of wasteful flurry; a
frenetic activity involving lots of different marketing
methods, such as organising PR; writing leaflets and paying
out lots of money for advertising campaigns offering very
uncertain results. This is an image often presented by the
press, eager to publish stories about marketing failures, and
is one that has found continual sympathy among traditional-
ists in the workforce unwilling to tolerate 'new fangled'
ideas.

True marketing is extremely logical. It means thinking
about your aims in detail and deciding how best to achieve
them.

How to check whether your market- ing is on track

Once you've mentally ticked the six statements above, how
can you check that your actual marketing is on track? If you
called in an external expert he or she would probably start by
asking you lots of questions, taking into account all product
and market factors. For example:

- What are your long- and short-term company objectives?

- What needs and opportunities does your market research
  reveal?

- How large is the demand for your product? Is it actual or
  potential? What is the competition doing?

- How long will it take you to research and develop an
  appropriate product?

- What does the market want it to look like?

- Where will you make it/get it made?

- How much should it cost?

- How will you tell the market about it?

- How many will you sell and how soon will it pay back your initial investment?

- How will you get it to the market?

- How will you know if your plans are succeeding?

- What else can you make or sell them if it does work?

It is the coordination of all these factors (or **synergy**) that constitutes effective marketing. Various marketing people have tried to condense these considerations into snappier, more memorable lists. For example, in the 1950s the Harvard Business School came up with the concept of the **marketing mix**. This consisted of getting the **right product** to the **right people** (the designated market) by **saying the right things** in the promotional message and **choosing the right way** (the creative strategy) at the **right time** and in the **right place** (sales vehicle or location).

The marketing mix, as classified by the **4 'P's,** was a system first advocated by E. J. McCarthy (see *Basic Marketing*, Further Reading) in 1954. He recommended that good marketing should pay attention to:

- product
- price
- place
- promotion

To this basic list others have added other important elements, such as personnel, profit and timing (period of time if you want to keep the Ps going!). It's also worth reordering these factors to reflect the primary importance of the customer. The list then looks like this:

- people
- product
- price
- promotion
- place
- (period of) time
- profit
- personnel

Let's look at these various elements in greater detail.

People

The market is made up of people whose needs are to be met. You have to identify different **market segments** (groups of customers with similar needs) and their specific needs, as well as the wider circle of potential buyers who might also be interested. A well-known rule of thumb (**Pareto's Law**) says that 80 per cent of your business will come from 20 per cent of your customers, and this rule seems to hold good throughout the life of a business, whether you recruit new customers or lose old ones. Whilst it is important to try to find new business, you should never do this at the expense of keeping the core of your customer-base satisfied.

Before any decisions are made you should carry out some market research. This should reveal where your customers are, the needs they have, and how to target them so that you do not waste time or money trying to reach those who are unlikely to be interested. (For more on market research, see Chapter 2.)

Product(s)

Your product is what you are going to devise/obtain to offer to your designated customers. In order to market your product successfully you need to consider the:

- specifications
- product benefits
- styling
- functions
- materials
- design and packaging (inner and outer)
- range and variety of products on offer
- deletions or additions to the range

All these elements should be considered in relation to what else is on the market; the direct and indirect competition. Some products are similar to each other ('me too' items such as soap powders); some are substitutes (a gas cylinder heated brush instead of plug-in heated rollers); others are completely new ways of dealing with existing or developing consumer requirements, often the result of extensive research and technological development (the disposable nappy instead of the cloth variety). All products are subsequently adapted and improved as the market develops, bearing in mind both developing consumer needs and the prevailing competition.

Price

Price setting is an immensely complicated subject. There are various methods of calculating product prices. All require you to think in detail about a number of questions:

- What are your overall marketing objectives? (Do you just want to survive, make a quick buck, or build a reputation for product quality?)

- How large is the demand and how long will it last? (The more stable the demand, the higher the price can be.)

- What does it cost to make your product and how long does it take to make?

- What are your other fixed and variable in-house costs?

- What are the competition producing and charging?

- What is the perceived value of the product? (The lowest possible price will not necessarily make it more attractive.)

- What is the most cost-effective quantity to produce?

- What is the break-even point? (How many do you have to sell to recoup your costs?) This helps you estimate the level of risk.

Then there are various pricing methods. Probably the best known method of price decision is **cost + x per cent**, where the production costs are established, an allowance made for overheads and then x per cent is added to achieve the desired profit margin. Other methods of pricing include **break-even analysis, target profit pricing, perceived value pricing, tender pricing** and **going rate pricing**.

Having decided on a price, it is important to express it in an attractive way that everyone understands, paying attention to **pricing points** above which a product will start to sound expensive, e.g. £9·99 not £10. Most direct mail markets offer an attractive price and then make postage and packing an additional cost; this sounds cheaper. The price must also be easy to understand. Prices such as £15 'non net', '£25 + VAT' or 'please add 15% for postage and packing' (leaving customers to work out the final total themselves) may make them wary of ordering. Not everyone has a calculator to hand or can do these sums in their heads: the resulting delay could cost you the order.

Whatever price setting method you use, the price should be part of the marketing strategy as a whole, not an afterthought. The price at which you offer a product is an *integral* part of the deal, not something that can be considered in isolation. The customer will not separate the product from its offer price; the two will stand – or fall – together. Also, the more you look outside your organisation when thinking about price setting (at the market, their needs and how you can meet them), the more likely you are to find a price that is attractive to the market and also enables you to make a profit. *Don't set prices in isolation from the market.*

Once you have set your selling price, you also need to establish your discounts, allowances, incentives, and how much credit you will give. You may wish to adopt individual pricing policies for particular products (e.g. start off with an introductory offer to encourage purchase, then push up the price when there is more demand. This gambit is often used when launching new cafés and restaurants). There may also be outstanding gaps in market segments for specific prices (e.g. Amstrad's launch, in the late 1980s, of a simplified (and cheaper) video recorder for households which already owned one such machine).

Promotion

The purpose of promotion is to generate profitable sales. Promotion is not another word for public relations; there should be a direct and measurable link between promotion and sales.

Promotional campaigns achieve their desired results by changing and/or directing the attitudes of the target audience: informing and persuading them; introducing them to the product and encouraging repeat purchase; expanding their numbers. This involves different promotional tools at different stages of the marketing process: perhaps a poster early on to shout a simple announcement, with a more detailed leaflet nearer launch time.

Promotions are aimed at trade customers (stockists); influencers (journalists, reviewers, opinion-formers such as chat show hosts and style leaders) and customers.

The **promotional mix** consists of both personal and impersonal methods. Impersonal promotional methods include:

- informational items (e.g. catalogues, leaflets, exhibitions)
- 'above the line' (e.g. paid for space advertising in newspapers and magazines)
- 'below the line' – mutually beneficial promotional deals between two or more advertisers (e.g. offering free holidays to shopkeepers as prizes for the best product displays)
- point of sale – advertising at the place where the product is paid for (e.g. posters and display material to be used in shops)
- free publicity and public relations (e.g. persuading the media to run features on your product)

Personal promotional methods include:

- sales representatives
- direct marketing (e.g. direct mail)

(For more on the promotional mix, see Chapters 4 and 8.)

Place

The place where you sell your product is another vital element in marketing it successfully. Consideration of place involves the physical movement of the goods to be sold: distribution. When deciding how to distribute your product you need to think about the following questions:

- Where are the goods to be stored?
- What sort of warehousing will you use? (Individual or cooperative?)
- What kind of outlets will the goods be sold through?
- How often will they need to be delivered?
- Will you have a minimum order size? Will you have small order surcharges?

- What method of delivery will you use?

- Will you make use of wholesalers?

- Will you have different customer service levels? (For example, free delivery for those who order in large quantities.)

These choices will depend on the nature of your customer base (how easy they are to reach and how they like to buy); the resources of the company (what you can afford); and the wider business situation (what other options you have for getting the product to the customer, e.g. door-to-door sales, party plans and so on). (For more on distribution, see Chapter 5.)

(Period of) Time

To get your timing right, you need to ask yourself the following questions:

- When does the market want to know about your products?

- When is the best time to organise the marketing?

- Are there seasonal variations in the market? (Will customers want to buy your summer clothes in mid-winter?)

- What are the in-house considerations? (When are your slack/busy periods?)

- Have you taken distributor/carrier schedules into account?

- What is the required schedule for exporting?

Profit

The most basic of economies is subsistence. A slight advance on this creates extra revenue which can be used for trade, and should ensure the continued growth of the local economy. Similarly in business, unless a product makes a profit, its survival is questionable; in the longer term the company itself may be threatened.

Revenue from selling your products should:

(a) cover the costs of the promotion

(b) cover the costs of the product research and production

(c) contribute to company overheads.

Profit is what is left once these costs have been covered.

Long-term and short-term profit aims also need to be compatible: will the short-term need to sell, in order to raise cash, prevent the company becoming more profitable in the long term? For example, an initial low price to encourage consumers to try a new product may reduce their appreciation of the product's value.

Profit also needs to be accountable. It must be measured in the part of the company where it originates, and according to the long-term expectations of different products. For instance, some products will only sell for a short period of time and therefore need to make a profit more quickly than those which are likely to sell for a number of years. General company profit levels are meaningless unless you know the source.

Personnel

Consider:

- your existing staff

- the staff you will need in the future

- who does what and whether there is any overlap

- the allocation of responsibility and control

- whether your staff need any additional training

- how and when to reward them

- how to make the best use of external consultants, recruit-

ment agencies and the personnel department to fill
temporary or permanent gaps

I have already mentioned the fact that marketing is a social
process, dependent on relationships both inside and outside
the firm. It follows that the people you employ are extremely
important. Marketing-orientated companies regard their
staff as one of their most important assets: they train and
motivate them and in return are rewarded with a more stable
workforce. This principle applies in whatever capacity they
are employed: distribution; production; or sales.

But whilst marketing involves all staff, there will be some
people in every company for whom the word 'marketing'
appears in their job title. Getting these appointments right is
particularly important, so the final section of this chapter
deals with how to find the right kind of people for specific
marketing jobs.

Advertisements for marketing staff usually contain certain
phrases, most of which relate to the six key elements of
marketing listed at the beginning of this chapter. For
example, you read of the need for marketing managers who
are 'self-starters', 'capable of motivating themselves and
others', 'innovators'. These are easy things to say; it is much
harder to spot the kind of person who is really able to deliver
the goods.

If you want an accountant you look for someone with the
right qualifications; the same, by and large, goes for choosing sales reps or receptionists. Good marketing people are
much harder to recognise through paper qualifications, other
than by, as American advertising agency boss, Raymond
Rubicam, instructed his copywriters: 'resisting the usual'.

Good marketing people are imaginative; advertising guru,
David Ogilvy, described their most important asset as an
'ungovernable curiosity'. They are enthusiastic and have a
great ability to get involved in what they are doing. They
have tangent minds and can see similarities where none
appear to the untrained eye; they are good at lateral thinking.
It follows therefore that the richer their experience of life to
date, the more they have to draw on in fulfilling your market-

ing aims. Following the same logic, a degree in an outlandish subject, time spent travelling to interesting places, and unusual hobbies, are all likely to breed a more interesting individual than single-minded devotion to a 'vocational' course (e.g. business studies or accountancy). David Ogilvy again: 'Talent, I believe, is more likely to be found among nonconformists, dissenters and rebels.'

Unfortunately today we seem to regard the development of an on-going and continually presentable CV as more important than an enquiring mind. It is difficult to say when the rot set in, but it seems to be a general trend in society that we are more interested in quantity than quality. The educational system in place today is so busy measuring performance that instilling a love of learning and developing an enquiring mind can get pushed into second place.

Those interviewing need to be clear about what they are looking for. Unfortunately it often happens that the people handling the selection for marketing jobs are not from a marketing background themselves. At the same time they are often wary of the candidates' articulateness and confidence and the very intangible skills they offer. These characteristics do not mean that they are unsuitable for the job. Far from it.

Today many firms approach interviewing very scientifically. They use psychometric testing (to understand the candidate's mental state) and graphology (handwriting analysis). This costs a lot of money and takes time. Here is a useful set of five quick questions to ask at an interview which should reveal whether your candidate has the kind of original mind you are looking for to fill a marketing job:

1 What brand of washing powder did your mother use when you were fifteen? What advertising slogan/image was used to promote it then?

2 Think of your five closest friends. What type of shoes does each one usually wear?

3 Which films are big box office successes at the moment? Which ones have you seen?

4 If you are a non-smoker, which brand of cigarette do you think has the best adverts? (For smokers, find a spirit they don't habitually drink and ask the same question.)

5 Think of the last time you went out for a meal. What did the person you went with have to eat? What were the people at the next table talking about?

There is a reason for all this. Enquiring minds store up trivia and parallels; they are good at spotting the context of the everyday world around them and can store the information for subsequent recall. They understand what makes one product different from another, both in product and image terms, and the associated competitive advantages one manufacturer thus has over another. All this gives them vast mental resources to draw on. One of the best copywriters I know excels at Trivial Pursuits.

Finally, having found some inventive and innovative minds for your marketing jobs, do motivate them! There is nothing more frustrating for creative people than bogging them down in administration; in management rather then problem-solving.

Large corporations are notoriously inward-looking; management can become an end in itself. Too often mid to senior management spend their working week doing nothing more creative than attending meetings; managing internal friction. And once people start directing their attention internally to improving their lot (usually through frequent reorganisations or bids to improve 'internal communications'), rather than furthering the company's external aims, nothing will ever make them happy; their demands will get bigger and bigger and any success will merely spur them on to the next fight.

Recognition is vital to the creative person; just as, if not more, important than money. There is nothing more ego-boosting (and, in job terms, motivating) than someone else taking your advice; even more so if they credit your contribution. Marketing people don't like to be bored, they need to keep having challenges thrown at them. In short, they may say they are looking for an easier life, but they aren't happy when they find it!

...ıeone say recently that he thought most
...ıning was a waste of time, as it filled candidates
...ɔrate bullshit' instead of making them think. This
... sweeping but there is certainly some truth in it.
Ma. .ting training too often emphasises the 'how' rather
than the 'why'. It's undoubtedly true that you can iron out
any amount of creativity by teaching slavish adherence to
rules, but you can never teach originality. Original minds are
born (and developed), not made.

And how often one hears of employees returning from
training courses to find that the new ideas their companies
have paid for them to hear are not part of the 'corporate
culture' and hence cannot be applied. This is extremely frustrating. The irony is that the employer ends up paying for the
employee to be given the motivation to start looking for
another job!

SUMMARY

Marketing means thinking about the customer. (If you remember nothing else from this book, please remember this one
sentence.)

Effective marketing cannot be achieved overnight and
works best when established over the long term, involving all
parts of the organisation. Long-term understanding of
marketing goals brings the ability to innovate and respond
successfully to the one certainty for any organisation:
change.

2

Market Research

Having decided to be market led rather than product led (i.e. producing what the market wants, rather than what the company knows how to produce), it is very important to *find out what the market does want*:

'... market research, together with the use of other trade or in-house information, is integral to the successful decision-making of any major consumer-based company today.'
Training Handbook of the Market Research Society

'It is a capital mistake to theorise before one has data.'
Sir Arthur Conan Doyle

The importance of market research has only been accepted by British industry fairly recently – most British companies did not start including it in their budgets until the end of the 1970s. But since then many company managers have realised the benefits of an independent, objective viewpoint and are using external market research companies much more readily.

What is market research?

Another definition. Market research aims to provide information to help companies decide on their product development and marketing strategies, including the exploration of both existing and potential markets. It enables companies to reduce uncertainty, monitor performance and make decisions. In other words, market research helps to show where a company's resources and efforts should be concentrated for most effect. It aims to understand the market in order to sell more effectively to it.

You cannot, however, assume that market research is infallible or able to provide answers to every problem. For example, the 1992 British general election was a disaster for researchers; all the polling companies bar one predicted a hung parliament days before the event. Research has a similarly uneven track record when it comes to predicting what will happen under changed circumstances (consumers rarely know themselves) or the future of completely new products. (When Akio Morito launched the highly successful Walkman personal stereo he did it in the face of prophecies of doom from market researchers.) Although good research should reveal pointers and trends, it is up to us to interpret the information and translate it into action.

Nor does the fact that you are setting up research programmes mean you should ignore the problem until you have your market research results. Not only should you be thinking about possible outcomes when determining how best to conduct the research, but – based on your existing understanding of your market – you should be considering your next step using **scenario generation** ('if we are seen as good on quality but poor on cost we will do x; if poor on quality and good on cost we will do y').

Bearing all these provisos in mind, a programme of market research should help you to:

1 Estimate the overall size and structure of the market, and see how it is currently divided up between existing products, services and outlets; find out what market share various brands have, and what **market segmentation** there is (different groups of consumers with similar needs, identified by social grade, demographic, ethnographic, psychographic (mental state) factors and so on).

2 Test your understanding of the market by providing feedback on how your own products/brands are perceived, thus putting you in a better position to predict future demand. Similarly, market research can provide feedback on how your marketing strategies are performing.

3 See opportunities and threats in the market.

4 Keep an eye on the competition, both direct and indirect, thus revealing how to offer a **competitive advantage** (what you can offer to the customer to make your product or service better or more appealing than that of your competitors), and hence where and how to 'position' a product.

5 Make logical and appropriate plans for the future.

6 Limit risk. (Marketing specialists estimate that 80 per cent of new products fail; for certain market sectors, like new restaurants, the failure rate is even higher. Hence the importance of thorough market research before any major investment takes place.)

Where does market research information come from?

It's not advisable to rush out on day one and instruct a bureau. You are more likely to get good results if you think about the kind of things you want to know and the likely sources of information before you start talking to the professionals. These sources include:

- personal experience
- internal records
- published industry-specific information
- other published information
- formal and specialist market research

Personal experience

This is often the starting point. New products and services are frequently inspired by personal experience: standing in queues or looking in vain for specific products can reveal a need. Scanning the shelves in shops and talking to sales assistants, friends and work colleagues may confirm whether or not other customers have similar needs and how they are currently served (or not).

Having identified a genuine need, consider whether you know any members of the primary market for your product personally. Do you know where they get together? Can you go along and talk to them or to those who buy on their behalf? If they are members of a specific profession, can you attend their annual conference or meetings of their professional organisation?

Internal records

Most companies have lots of market information that can be analysed and quantified into trends. For example there are customer lists; accounts department statistics; sales records; year-on-year statistics; mailing responses from previous campaigns; telemarketing (in- and out-bound); reports from reps and the distribution centre; customer letters/complaints/warranty and guarantee claims; feedback from EPOS (electronic point of sale) in retail outlets.

Published industry-specific information

In many industries individual firms provide sales data to show how their various products are selling. Taken together, this information should give you a reasonably accurate idea of the overall size of the market. The size of both the car and drugs industries can be estimated in this way. Similarly, government statistics provide useful market information, as do regular surveys from those producing industry commentaries (e.g. Mintel, Euromonitor and the Government Household Surveys, and similar studies from other countries). Other industry-specific market information comes from the trade press, newspapers and professional journals, and figures in other relevant reference sources such as company reports and feedback from professional associations.

Other published information

Then there are all the different sorts of information assembled for one use but relevant to another. For example, reports on the fastest-growing subjects for students at GCSE and 'A'-level would be very useful to an educational publisher. Likewise, Department of Health statistics on the prevalence of particular dietary problems would be very useful to a manufacturer of special foods.

There is a whole range of information that is relevant, even if it is not specifically applicable to target markets, e.g. government statistics and surveys; industry association sources; membership of cooperative industry research surveys. Such information may be purchased or is sometimes available free.

Formal and specialist market research

This can be organised in-house by allocating new or existing members of staff or externally through agencies or specialists. Some firms use a combination of the two.

Some specialist market research organisations operate in particular market sectors, while others are generalists. Even if you can't afford your own market research programme, most large agencies (Gallup, NOP, SRA, etc) run regular cooperative questionnairing programmes aimed at both general and specific markets (such as household or children's interests). BRMB International run the Target Group Index (TGI), which is a survey of about 24,000 households, asking about their lifestyle, their purchase of a huge range of products and services, and their use of various media.

A word of warning

While desk research, personal experience and observation are all valuable ways of gathering information (and thus preventing time and money being wasted on repeating what is already available), great care must be taken when drawing conclusions from the information obtained. You will need to consider the reliability and objectivity of such data; the comparability of information obtained from several sources; the question of whether there was some particular 'political' motive for publishing or stressing certain points; and watch out for 'opinion' dressed up as 'fact'. Even government statistics are far from complete or reliable – they are frequently adjusted several times after publication, often quite radically.

Different methods of market research

First, a bit of jargon. Most market research is one of two sorts. As you will hear these terms bandied around quite a bit, it's important to understand the difference between **qualitative** and **quantitative** market research.

Qualitative research aims to assess the breadth of opinions and behaviour, but not the extent to which opinions are held or the numbers who behave in particular ways. Quantitative research tries to determine how many people – and of what sort – behave in particular ways, or hold certain opinions, or buy particular products, and so on. Generally, in quantitative research the aim is to obtain an overall picture of the market, but not to go too deeply into motivations and attitudes. In qualitative research the aim is to look at the psychological aspects more closely, without trying to assume how the market as a whole works.

These two types of research are often used in combination, and it is often difficult to know whether a project is one or the other. There are large and small-scale projects for both, and the difference is frequently more theoretical than real.

In terms of sheer expenditure through research agencies, more money gets spent on quantitative than qualitative projects – though almost certainly there are more of the lattter than the former. However, many companies feel able to carry out smaller-scale qualitative studies of their own – in particular business-to-business or trade research – and so the total real cost of qualitative research may well equal that of quantitative.

There are various different methods of conducting market research. Their respective value depends on the nature of the population being targeted and the most effective method of reaching them. The 'target population' does not necessarily only consist of actual or potential customers (trade or consumer); equally important are those who consume the product but do not buy it (e.g. in most families one person buys the toothpaste but it must satisfy all the different members). There are also those who have it in their power to recommend the product without necessarily buying it themselves (e.g. shop assistants and children).

Selecting the correct respondents to interview is, of course, vital. In qualitative research, recruiters are usually asked to start by finding people who fulfil specific criteria, both demographic (e.g. by age, sex, class, area) and product-related (do/don't buy a particular brand). Such people are then asked to take part in the project.

In quantitative research a decision has to be taken as to what representation of which populations is required. For instance, the sample could be taken to be representative of the adult population as a whole, and selection will either be by quota (e.g. 45 per cent men, 20 per cent under 30) or by random selection. True random sampling is very expensive and thus very rare these days. Most sampling uses a mixture of quota and random methods.

Some quantitative surveys are deliberately biased in their sample selection, to ensure sufficient numbers of particular respondent types are interviewed for realistic statistical analysis.

Questions are then asked through:

- telephone surveys
- questionnaires completed by individuals (either conducted house-to-house, or delivered/handed out with a purchase, completed in the recipient's own time and returned either by post or through electronic transfer)
- face-to-face interviews carried out in-store/location, in the street or in the home
- 'mall' or 'hall' tests (a group of people gathered together and asked for their opinions)
- group discussions
- panel research (a group of people recruited to provide information from time to time, on an ad hoc or more formal basis, or both, such as BBC Radio's Panel of Listeners)

What kind of information is revealed?

Market research can provide data on performance and behaviour (what is happening in the market). It can answer the following questions:

- Who buys what, in what quantity and where from?
- What are the shopping habits/spending power of those buying?
- Who is buying and who is not buying?
- What sizes and variations are being bought?
- What is the overall size of the market?
- Is the market growing or contracting?
- Is the market contactable/accessible?

- Which products are being bought (best-selling versus others)?

- In what quantities?

- How fast are they selling?

- What are the buying patterns by market segment?

- How are they used and how do they perform?

- What stock levels are being held in trade outlets (e.g. shops)?

- What stock levels are being held in wholesale and other distribution outlets?

Market research can also give us data on attitude and motivation, answering questions such as:

- How is the choice actually made by the customer? What are the primary and secondary influences?

- Why do they buy?

- How will they use the product or service?

- What is the market's reaction to the company image?

Market research can also reveal information on how best to sell to the market, such as:

- How can the marketing message best be put across?

- What are the most appropriate messages or types of promotion to use?

What does market research cost and how cost-effective is it?

John Samuels, Managing Director of BRMB International, commented that less than 0·2 per cent of the cost of production is typically spent by manufacturing companies on market research. Some industries spend a great deal more on market research, e.g. pharmaceutical companies, banks, insurance and other financial sector firms, drink and car manufacturers. It is probably also true that larger companies spend a higher proportion on research than smaller ones, although there are no reliable figures for this.

Most firms with no experience of using market research assume they can't afford it. Others who are using it realise they can't afford not to. The skill (unless you have a limitless budget) is only spending money on finding out things you really need to know.

A word of warning. Do not assume that in-house market research will always be cheaper (even though the costs may be covered by several contributory budgets or even informally disguised). External services offer the advantage of trained personnel, experienced in this kind of work; they should be objective and free from preconceived ideas about a particular market or opportunity. If you haven't been involved in market research before, it's unlikely that you will have any experience of designing appropriate market research vehicles to find out what you want to know.

If you use a badly designed survey – or more obviously, a badly designed and worded questionnaire – the results may either not tell you what you need to know or be totally misleading, resulting in false assumptions being fed into the decision-making process. In addition, for security reasons, it may be better to use an external organisation to screen the identity of the questioner. It is often easier, too, for external agencies to maintain respondent confidentiality, thus promoting greater freedom (and hence honesty) in response.

How to get value for money from market research

All market research can be cost effective if it is designed to address the marketing and sales issues concerned.

Robin Birn

1 Be precise about what you want to know

Avoid 'paralysis by analysis'. Research revealing absolutely everything about a market would probably not be possible or useful, and certainly not affordable! Data for data's sake is rarely worth while; it is better to plan the collection of information into a continuous marketing information system (perhaps by allocating responsibility to one individual within a department for circulating and storing information likely to be of general interest).

2 Use the right vehicle (and lots of common sense)

Don't employ an agency to tackle something in-house staff have easy access to. And if you decide to employ professionals, make sure they are the right kind of professionals. I heard of a firm recently who commissioned market research from management consultants who charged about three times what a specialist research agency would have quoted.

3 Pay attention to any trends that are identified

Market research is normally only cost-effective if it is carefully designed to meet particular needs at a specific time (often marketing or sales or product development), and the resulting conclusions are acted upon. It's also important to respond to any information coming back now from your existing marketing programme (e.g. which leaflets produce the best results, what price promotions the reps find yield the best results, and so on).

4 Take a long-term view

Although market research can be used successfully for short-term tactical purposes, it probably works best if you are willing to take a long-term view of your company and its products. The companies who make the best use of the information are those who build market research into their planning and marketing processes, and don't only use it as a means of obtaining answers to short-term problems.

5 And finally, don't expect the earth

Remember that market research is not infallible, and your interpretation and action on findings matter more than the research itself.

Wasted market research is usually due to one of the following avoidable reasons:

- inadequate briefing

- inappropriate survey design

- neglect of available information sources

- poor communications (e.g. ambiguous questions)

- biased or inadequate interpretation

- lack of ownership of the survey/data (somebody should want it done and act as the sponsor)

How to find a market research firm

If you are considering commissioning market research from a supplier, a useful first port of call is the *Orgs Book*, produced annually by the Market Research Society (see Useful Addresses). Here you will find listed a variety of organisations and individuals providing market research services; their size and turnover; specialisations, previous experience and key personnel. Membership of the Society is open to individuals and there are now around 7,000 elected members who have met the selection criteria and have agreed to abide by the Society's Code of Conduct.

Before approaching the firms and individuals detailed in the book, it is helpful if you have already prepared the following information, preferably in the form of a written brief:

- the research problem(s) that you want solved

- background information on your organisation, so that the market research firm can see the problem in context

- information on what use the market research data is likely to be put to; what kind of decisions it will influence

- a broad indication of the budget available

Another extremely useful source of information is AURA – the Association of Users of Research Agencies (see Useful Addresses). This body includes many of the major client companies who get together to discuss issues of importance and exchange information about research agencies and consultants. They operate as a network, asking advice from their colleagues about whom to use for different types of project. Membership is open to companies of all sizes and covers most industries.

Should you approach more than one firm?

Market research companies will often spend a considerable amount of time preparing proposals for possible new clients. It is therefore good practice only to approach them on a formal basis when there is a reasonable probability that the project you are discussing will actually be commissioned. If you decide to commission through competitive tender, those submitting tenders should be aware of the situation and you should restrict the firms being approached to a reasonable number (say two to four).

Examples of market research in action

Formal market research

With the crime fiction market buoyant in 1985, publishers HarperCollins found that sales of their brand leader Agatha Christie were declining – by around 1 per cent a year. Market research was commissioned from James R. Adams and Associates to find out why, and a mixture of desk research, qualitative and quantitative research was suggested.

The market for her titles was found to be biased towards the young, the better educated and those from higher socio-economic groups. Group discussions amongst existing Christie readers and current paperback buyers were set up; views from all socio-economic grades and both sexes were sought.

The most interesting finding to emerge was that Christie readers like the 'niceness' of the crimes; there may be a whole series of violent deaths in her books, but there is no dwelling on the details. However the rather gory covers (influenced by the growing horror market) put these readers off.

As a direct result of the research, new cover designs, both intriguing and subtle, were commissioned and a new promotion of Agatha Christie as the 'Queen of Crime' received widespread support from the book trade. In the first year after making the changes, paperback sales increased by 40 per cent (1m up to 1·4m units).

Any business involved in selling through mail order is carrying out market research at the same time. Sales figures reveal which products and services sell best, when, and in what combinations. What you often don't find out is why other things *don't* sell.

Jim Martin, Managing Director of the N. Brown Group, a large mail order company (estimated to have clothed and shod 1·5 million women in Britain in 1993), wanted to know why so many mail order items were returned.

To find out, he paid Manchester University £100,000 to take 70 different measurements from each of more than 700 women. Two years – and 50,000 measurements – later, the university research team came up with the answer: women are apparently bigger, wider and differently shaped than they were just after the Second World War when sizes were standardised. 'They've got thicker waists, lower busts and their figures are more conical than hour glass,' Jim Martin commented. As a result, today only one woman in ten finds a standard fitting suitable. Martin's response was to launch a new range of clothes, 'Classic Combinations', based on these new vital statistics. So far the range is selling well, and he claims a sharply reduced returns rate – now 27 per cent against an industry average of 35 per cent.

Informal market research

The founders of Blooming Marvellous, a company supplying maternity wear by direct mail, drew their initial market research from their own experience – there was no one selling attractively designed, reasonably priced maternity wear. Further enquiries amongst their contemporaries and friends confirmed their instincts and they developed their first products to serve this market – simple sweatshirts with amusing captions on them.

Offering these to their basic market of pregnant women provided both orders and further sources for market research – information on what locations for advertising material worked best (magazine ads worked, handouts in antenatal clinics didn't), what colours and sizes were most popular, and what seasons were most profitable.

Today the two founders continue to run a successful mail order company, now incidentally employing over 40 people. Central to the business is a sophisticated computer software package that was originally developed for US mail order companies. It can hold hundreds of thousands of customer records and maintain very good information on stock levels. Market research gained from both customer orders and letters from satisfied (and, on occasion, dissatisfied) customers continues to be fundamental to the business, both in planning new product lines and developing new markets.

For broadcast programmes, the customers are the listeners and viewers, but without market research it can be very difficult to judge how many there are. There are ongoing surveys to establish the 'ratings', but one-off promotions can be very revealing.

For example, sex therapist Dr Ruth Westheimer began her broadcasting career with a ten-minute late-night slot on New York Radio discussing couples' sexual problems. It was only when a sweatshirt was offered to listeners, and a huge response came in, that the broadcasting station realised quite how many people were tuning in. The result was that her spot was moved to a slightly earlier time, and extended. A syndicated television series followed and her newspaper columns are now syndicated in over 100 editions worldwide.

SUMMARY

If marketing centres on the customer, it follows that market research – to reveal the customers' needs, values and spending patterns – is very important.

Market research can be gathered from a wide variety of sources, both formal and informal. However, once acquired, it does not automatically ensure success. Its findings must always be interpreted in the light of the commissioner's experience, market understanding and personal instincts.

3

The Marketing Plan

A S WE HAVE already seen, to be really effective, marketing needs to be a long-term operation. This starts most logically with planning, and so this chapter is devoted to the mechanics of drawing up a marketing plan.

If asked to come up with a marketing plan most people would probably start by making a list of the practical activities to be included, such as where and when to advertise or whom to mail with a brochure, or the practical results to be achieved, with a forecast of sales or budget for marketing expenditure. But whilst these are all important parts of any plan, the reality is much more complex. Just as marketing itself takes nothing for granted – shaping the product to the needs of the market – so the marketing plan needs to be equally wide in scope and outward-looking.

A word of warning before we start. The process of planning, and the objective analysis that should accompany it, is more important than the eventual plan itself. The marketing plan should produce strategies to achieve specified aims, but the plan must never become an end in itself. If you concentrate on the plan alone you may end up with inertia (just like revision plans for exams that made you feel you had done all the work and need do nothing more).

The various stages of the marketing plan

A comprehensive marketing plan can usefully be divided up into stages, each of which I will examine in further detail. In reality some stages are skipped and some occur at the same time but they nevertheless form a useful model for explanation. Here they are:

1 Agree the overall goal.

2 Carry out an internal audit to identify your own strengths and weaknesses.

3 Carry out an external audit to identify opportunities and threats.

4 Do a SWOT analysis.

5 Set marketing objectives and strategy.

6 Communicate the plan to your staff.

7 Measure the success of the plan.

1   Agree the overall goal

A company or an individual needs to know where it is going; an organisation that is directionless will get nowhere.

Before you can establish objectives, you need to understand *what business you are working in.* Management consultants charge large fees for helping you to answer this question; it's cheaper to start thinking about it yourself. Here are some examples. A firm supplying sandwiches to offices in Central London is in the hunger business and could usefully extend its activities into providing office catering for special functions. Garage owners are in the transport business, and in addition to offering related transport products (such as fuel and car hire), many have developed stores that offer all kinds of other goods to the travelling public, snacks, drinks, audio-tapes and so on. Others have developed their standing in the convenience business: garages are often open 24 hours a day, and many now sell bulky or heavy items that are conveniently bought by car, such as barbecue fuel, garden furniture and plastic storage containers.

It is equally interesting to spot organisations that have been stranded by time because they did *not* realise what business they were in. Failing to recognise that the market was changing, they made no attempt to adapt their product or service to those changes. For example, the railroad industry in America saw itself as providing rail services rather than transportation, and so lost out to road and air freight services. European piano-makers are in the business of home entertainment, not music. The technological development of electronic pianos which are portable and require no tuning has entirely passed them by, and has been exploited, in the main, by the Japanese.

The result of deciding what business you are in and thinking about what you want to achieve within that industry is generally called a **mission statement**. This may sound like something from *Star Trek* but it is very important. Your mission statement is your *raison d'être*; it says where a firm or an individual wants to go; it charts 'a journey with a purpose'. Again, some examples:

'Young & Rubicam's mission is to be its clients' most valuable partner, helping them build, leverage and manage their brand assets, whether product or corporate.'

YOUNG & RUBICAM FACTS AND FIGURES 1993

'Our vision is to be a vibrant church making Jesus Christ known to all on Kingston Hill, seven days a week.'

ST PAUL'S CHURCH, KINGSTON HILL

'I want to have achieved a sufficient position within my company so that by the age of 30 I can give up my job, move out of London and have children.'

A mission statement doesn't need to be bound in maroon

leather – indeed it can be scribbled on the back of an envelope – but it *must* be understood by everyone in the
organisation. Writing it down is important – it helps crys-
tallise your ideas and serves as the basis for communicating
it to others. It also helps you focus on the 'job in hand',
preventing you from changing your mind from week to week
or being distracted from your own agenda. As political corre-
spondent Andrew Marr wrote in an obituary of John Smith,
Leader of the Labour Party (*Independent*, 13 May 1994):
'Faced by the media demanding instant policy, a political
agenda subservient to the news agenda, he was infuriatingly
passive. He was keeping his eye on the long term, thank you.'

Before arriving at a mission statement, it is obviously very
important to analyse your strengths and weaknesses (Where
are we? Where are we going? How are we going to get
there?). Equally important is a sense of determined excite-
ment in creating your mission statement; unless you have the
desire to get somewhere, you are unlikely to arrive.

The mission statement is based on:

- the history of the company

- the resources available

- the special skills or services offered by the company

- the external business environment (i.e. factors over which
  you have no control)

- the aims of current management

It defines:

- the market segment (group of customers) you are
  targeting

- the type of product or service to be promoted

- the scale of your objectives

- your financial objectives

- the timescale over which you seek to fulfil your objectives

Mission statements can be further condensed into slogans so that everyone knows what a specific company stands for. For instance 'Good food costs less at Sainsburys' conveys the quality and price advantage that lies at the heart of their marketing. (This slogan has since been dropped, but most of the general public have yet to notice!)

Once you've got a mission statement, don't just stick it in a drawer and forget about it! A mission statement should be a document that enthuses people about where they are going, and an organisational manifesto that sets the firm moving in the right direction.

If based on realistic assessments of your current business, the mission statement can be broken down into achievable objectives for both the company and the individuals working there. A firm's objectives for its corporate future and individual employees need to be in sympathy. They should be based on skills available, past experience and understanding of the market.

For example, a food manufacturing company's corporate objective, couched in a mission statement, might be to become a market leader in the potato crisp field. This could be broken down into individual objectives corresponding to the job responsibilities/needs/talents of those working for the company. In this case, the corporate goal would be served by setting up an enhanced potato crisp department, for which the potential senior managers were already available.

It is also vital to reconcile long-term strategic planning with short-term operational planning. For example, reducing staff in the customer services department may save money in the short term, but in the long run leads to the loss of more money in missed sales.

Once you have a clear idea of what your organisation is trying to do, it's vital to take a long cool look at the resources and opportunities you have available to achieve it. This is known as the marketing audit. There are several main areas to examine: existing internal factors which are under your control (this is the **internal audit**) and external factors over which you have no control, including the prevailing economic conditions and the competition (this is the **external audit**).

2 Carry out an internal audit to identify your own strengths and weaknesses

Let's start by establishing how marketing-orientated your particular organisation currently is.

Marketing-orientated companies look outwards not inwards; they focus on their own strengths, the external environment, the competition and the customer. Here is a checklist of eight different marketing considerations. Give your company a score out of ten for their marketing orientation in each area:

- Does your company focus primarily on customers or products?

- How clearly are individual departmental objectives understood and adopted?

- What effort is made to accumulate customer information?

- Assess the extent of organisation and investment in customer information.

- What is the depth of knowledge and focus on the competition?

- Assess the level of resourcing (staff and budget) for marketing activities.

- How much marketing expertise is there in the company?

- Are employees rewarded in relation to their marketing orientation?

The maximum possible score is 80. Carried out as a confidential exercise on marketing courses, I have seldom seen figures above the mid-40s. The average score is usually around 32.

Another way of assessing marketing orientation is examining who gets involved. Who considers the needs of the customer as part of their job function?

It's very important to state right now that *everyone* should. Marketing is about the customer, so everyone in your company should be aware of how the customer perceives your organisation, what they want, and what you can supply to fulfil their needs. Marketing is not the preserve of the marketing department! It involves everyone, from receptionist and post manager to senior management.

Now to the marketing audit. What assets do you have in-house? Your evaluation should include consideration of the following **internal marketing variables**:

- What are your present sales and market share?

- What is your profit margin? (What does it cost to make a sale? What is the level of profit on each sale?)

- What are your marketing procedures? (What procedures are already established and how effective are they?)

- What staff do you have available?

- Where is their effort principally directed? (Watch out for internal hierarchies and office politics which can impede the main thrust of the organisation.)

- What market information do you have?

- What resources/special advantages can you offer the market? (Perhaps a reputation for quality or a particularly well-briefed sales force?)

- What are your weaknesses? (Perhaps distribution or customer service?)

- What can you do about them?

- How do you compare with the competition?

- Do you have sufficient resources to achieve your aims?

- What additional strengths/structures do you need in-house to achieve your aims?

- And what risks are involved in making these changes?

3   Carry out an external audit to identify opportunities and threats

The external audit explores factors which the company has no direct control over but must nevertheless take into account. There are three main areas to look at: the external market variables; the business and economic environment; and the competition.

Firstly, the **external market variables** establish the shape of the current market and your place within it. You need to ask the following questions:

- What are market conditions like?

- How big is the market? (Is it growing or contracting?)

- What products are available and at what prices?

- How easy is it to reach the market (to distribute and communicate)?

Secondly, you need to look at the business and economic environment, considering the economic, political, social and technological factors. For example, the economic outlook may be encouraging but will recent EC legislation removing import bans affect your market penetration? A rising birth-rate may increase the market for your goods but will new technology – and hence cheaper manufacturing costs – lead to lower-priced competition?

Thirdly, you have to assess the competition by asking:

- Who are your competitors?
- How big are they?
- What is their market share?
- What are their production capabilities?
- How effective is their distribution?
- What marketing methods do they use?
- What is the extent of their diversification (their range of products, services etc)?

- What are their key strengths and weaknesses?

- What are their plans for the future?

Competitors are not necessarily companies producing a rival product for exactly the same purpose. For example, manufacturers of chocolate and snacks are worried about competition from the National Lottery, fearing that consumers' disposable income could be diverted from confectionery to lottery tickets. One major confectionery firm (Cadburys) is a member of the consortium running the lottery (Camelot). Similarly, all kinds of manufacturers, from cosmetics and accessories companies to book publishers and wine merchants, compete for the gift market. If your competitors' production costs are lower then your own they will be better placed to survive, should there be a price war.

For all these reasons, your firm should have a detailed understanding of the competition and be aware of their: main products, brands, ranges and so on; advertising, mailing and exhibitions; rep activity (feedback from your own is very useful here); job advertising; corporate public relations and image.

It is possible to pay a press agency, such as Romeike and Curtice (see Useful Addresses), to gather relevant news and advertisement clippings for you, but preferable to do this in-house. Sources of competition are not always advertised in a consistent manner.

4 Do a SWOT analysis

Having carried out an extensive internal and external audit, you should be able to identify four key areas:

- Internal **S**trengths

- Internal **W**eaknesses

- External **O**pportunities

- External **T**hreats

This information is known as a SWOT analysis, and is usually laid out in the form of a chart. Here is a SWOT analysis for a woman approaching 30 who is planning to leave London, start a family and give up work:

- **Strengths**
  Both partners want children.
  No evidence of inherited genetic disease.
  Sufficient income generated by one partner to support a family.

- **Weaknesses**
  She may not be happy at home all day when she has always worked.
  Living on one income will reduce their standard of living.

- **Opportunities**
  The company she works for is asking for voluntary redundancies.
  A large house would cost much less outside London.
  Freelance work may be available.

- **Threats**
  Female fertility decreases with age, while the chance of birth defects increases.

A clear SWOT analysis helps you pinpoint both your strong and weak points, converting uncertainty into risk, which can then be estimated.

Consider the short- and long-term consequences of success and failure? Financial loss is an obvious factor, but corporate credibility and reputation also need to be considered.

How much investment is required before a project will start to earn money, and when will it start to yield a profit? Are existing income sources sufficient to fund investment until then? Are the long-term profit possibilities worth the risk of the initial investment? Will there still be a demand for the new product in ten years' time or will social trends and technological developments render it obsolete?

Managements need to beware of the tendency of powerful

personalities within the company to make self-fulfilling prophecies of failure. Examining risk in detail helps avoid this.

5   Set marketing objectives and strategy

Setting objectives and strategies are key stages in formulating a marketing plan. Marketing objectives are the goals you want to achieve (what and why?). Marketing strategies are the ways you set about achieving them (who, where, when and how?).

The marketing objectives involve matching products and markets. You have four main options (together known as **Ansoff's matrix**):

- selling existing goods to existing markets
- selling existing goods to new markets
- developing new goods for existing markets
- developing new goods for new markets

Different marketing responses are needed for each option. Of course reality is never as simple as this matrix implies, but it is clear that the riskiest options involve developing new goods and new markets, because these take you away from your existing area of expertise.

Marketing strategies are the means by which you achieve your marketing objectives, by utilising the basic elements of the marketing mix (people, product, price, promotion, place, period of time, profit and personnel, as discussed in Chapter 1). The way you apply these different elements will depend on:

- the nature of the product and the customers
- how the market finds it convenient to buy/hear about new products
- how large a budget has been allocated for promotion

- whether you are selling direct to customers or expecting orders to come through a third party (i.e. how high a discount you will have to give).

All the different promotional techniques should be coordinated to achieve a synergy (each part of the organisation functioning in its own right and together helping to promote a consistent image of the whole company). Marketing-orientated companies are flexible; they adapt as market conditions change, or preferably just before they change, having anticipated the way the market is moving.

To illustrate the various stages outlined so far, here is a brief marketing plan for a new firm, The Wykeham Transport Company (WTC), planning to offer a low-cost transport business in the Winchester area.

1   Overall goal

This new service is in the transport business, offering a low-cost alternative to the large, national removal and haulage companies. With lower overheads and part-time staff, it can be very competitive on price, offering customers both a good deal and a local service.

MISSION STATEMENT: At the WTC we aim to provide flexible solutions to all the market's transport problems; to be friendly, efficient and available when needed so that the market comes to rely on us and think of us first.

2   Internal marketing audit

The proprietor owns one large van outright and, when needed, can secure others on very good terms at short notice. His family are willing to work in the business too, doing the accounts and taking bookings when he is out on the road. Having worked for one of the larger haulage companies he knows a lot about the transport business; having been recently made redundant he is determined to make this business work.

3 External marketing audit

External market conditions are favourable. The 'car boot sale mentality' that now pervades Britain means that everyone is looking for a better deal. Some grants and training are available to individuals setting up small businesses. The competition consists of larger removal companies and haulage companies offering much the same service. Both types of company are better organised, better funded and better known, but they are also perceived as expensive and inflexible. There is little overlap between the two main competitors; the WTC can offer both strings to its bow.

4 SWOT analysis

Internal strengths

- commitment of owner
- low operating costs
- flexibility. The WTC can move any sort of load – household or haulage
- people perceive a one-man operation as cheaper and are likely to favour using him for smaller-scale jobs
- local appeal

Internal weaknesses

- overwork; the owner can't be everywhere at once
- heavily reliant on hiring extra labour when needed – will the owner be able to find the standard he requires when he wants them?
- will his family get fed up with the business and want to do something else?
- no storage facilities at present

External opportunities

- improving transport network
- housing market is picking up again; the signs are that prices are finally rising a little, thereby encouraging people to move

External threats

- the larger removal companies may decide to invest in this end of the market too

- the growing availability of hire and drive-yourself options

- the owner may not be considered for jobs he could easily handle because perceived as 'too small'

- forthcoming general election may nip the house-moving spirit in the bud

5   Marketing objectives and strategy

The marketing objective is to let target markets know about the new service. Such key markets include:

- those moving house or thinking about doing so

- those advising them

- sale-rooms and auction houses selling heavy-duty items, such as furniture and machinery

- dealers arranging house clearances and liquidation sales

- retailers selling similar items who either do not have their own transport facilities or find them at times overloaded

The marketing strategy is to get the message across to the target market. Strategies could include:

- printing business cards and circulating, preferably by personal contact or recommendation, to: estate agents in the region; local solicitors; auction houses; dealers in furniture; local shops selling bulky merchandise, e.g. furniture, garden supplies; and anyone who has used the service in the hope that they will pass on the name to other relevant contacts. Cards could be sent out with invoices, estimates and any other form of customer contact. They could, at very low cost, be put on notice boards in shops and libraries and given out at Citizen Advice Bureaux.

- low-cost advertising in local directories, such as *Yellow Pages* and *The Thompson Directory*.

6 Communicate the plan to your staff

Communication and a determination to carry out the plan decided upon are vital; without them nothing will happen. The Army trains officers to think of a plan in three stages. Firstly they decide on their aims and work out how to achieve them; secondly they communicate the plan; and thirdly they see it through.

Don't forget how important internal communication is. Most firms have an internal circulation procedure for keeping all those who need to know, informed. But the people least often on the circulation list are those who most need to know what is going on. Don't forget the key role of those who can turn stray calls and enquiries into orders – your post managers or telephonists, or other staff who may answer your telephone. If you involve all your staff in your goals they will take a personal pride in working towards them.

7 Measure the success of the plan

Most firms set three- or five-year targets, update annually, and then break their aims down into yearly plans of action and anticipated results.

Contingency, or 'what if' plans, are important, as is deciding how soon to cut your losses. The ability to recognise early signs of failure and react quickly can rescue a difficult situation. For example, it is not necessary to count every returned order before deciding whether or not a mailing is successful; for most there is a half-life point, at which the total outcome can be predicted. Cereal manufacturers can judge the success of a promotion on the back of a packet within a couple of weeks of its launch. Similarly, food manufacturers often test new products in specific regions (usually linked to television areas) before taking a product nationwide. This way they can establish what political commentators after the 1993 election might have called the 'Basildon syndrome'!

If a product becomes a success, that success is usually

ascribed to its excellence. Failures are less easily 'under-stood', moreover there is an entirely natural reluctance amongst individuals to get involved – and hence identified with – things that have gone wrong. What is more, the sheer speed at which products succeed or fail can mean that there is often little time for formal analysis. Lessons tend to be carried around in the heads of senior management who then air their prejudices if a similar project crops up in the future.

Beyond this informal reaction to sales patterns, there are various systems for measuring the effectiveness of marketing. Most companies have reporting systems of some kind, but not all provide sufficient information to deduce whether the activity is profitable, or which areas need improvement.

There are three main types of system. **Annual targets** are used to measure performance against prediction. **Moving standards** (e.g. monthly sales totals) are used to do the same. And **diagnostic standards** give continuous feedback on market factors by constantly monitoring how the market is reacting to the campaign. Now that the technology exists, at a relatively low price, to chart these factors, principally through EPOS (electronic point of sale), more companies can benefit from such information. These are the standards by which large retail outlets, such as supermarket chains, are already making decisions on whether or not to stock a partic-ular item.

Here are some examples of ways in which diagnostic stan-dards can be used:

- measuring volume, growth and speed of sales, not just totals

- monitoring how accurately schedules are adhered to

- monitoring actual output against marketing plan

- year-on-year studies (of sales figures, marketing activities etc)

- checking whether the amount and percentage of business with major accounts is year-up or year-down; and subse-quently discussing market share with these accounts to try to influence the pattern, in return for incentives

- estimating your own market share and that of your major competitors

- estimating the number of repeat sales, complaints and returns levels

- monitoring delivery times, and comparing them with those of your competitors

- carrying out studies to estimate customer satisfaction

- understanding how your different brands are viewed by the market

- examining sales figures before and after major promotions (this is particularly important if responses to your mailings can come back via the retail trade rather than directly to you)

- counting the coupons/responses to particular mailings and comparing with similar products/market predictions

Information that comes back from the market needs to be assimilated, understood and formatted in a meaningful way. This will help you forecast market potential and market share and organise your business to cope with likely changes in demand. Reactive information (from customer questionnaires, feedback from customer relations departments, etc) and non-reactive information (such as stored sales data) should all be collected, systematised and analysed. For specific advice on setting up an in-house database, see Chapter 8, page 170.

SUMMARY

Preparing a marketing plan helps you establish the strengths and weaknesses of your market position, both internally (such as your staff and premises) and externally (taking into account prevailing political and economic factors that are likely to affect your business). However, as market condi-

tions change all the time, establishing a system of methodi-
cally charting, and deciding how to respond to, the relevant
market factors is just as important as formulating the overall
plan.

4

The Promotional Mix

WE HAVE ALREADY established the fact that if you do not produce what the customer wants you are likely to go out of business. But, even if you are producing the right products, unless you get your sales message across to the target market you still risk failure. *How* to get your message across is the subject of this chapter.

The sales message is transmitted to the target market through a number of different methods which together make up the **promotional mix**. These various techniques are what most people think of as marketing: practical activities, such as writing press releases, preparing catalogues and briefing sales reps. It is essential to match the promotional technique to the market being approached.

However, before you decide on the promotional mix or the right channel of communication, you will need to:

- identify the target audience
- decide what message you are trying to get across
- design the message
- work out the total promotional budget
- decide on the timing

Having made these decisions and worked out your promotional mix, you will also have to:

- forecast the results of the promotion

● establish how you will measure the results and decide if corrective action is needed

● work out contingency plans and revised forecasts

Before you start, it's worth thinking about what you are up against. Firstly, there are very few simple buying decisions today. Even staple commodities are available in a huge variety of different forms. To take a very simple example, think of the humble egg. We can choose between free range and battery, and perchery, a sort of in-between version. Then we can decide on the basis of egg size, colour, type of packaging (plastic or cardboard) and quantity (6, 10, 12, 18, 24 or 36 in a pack), with corresponding reductions in price per egg if you buy a larger quantity. All the labelling informing our choice must conform to both UK and EC legislation, and there are now sell-by dates for the consumer to examine as well. When you start considering the purchase of items such as cars or clothing, which are available in a huge variety of styles, colours, and so on, buying decisions become extremely complicated. What is more, each of these decisions takes place against the background of a huge amount of marketing information; promotional messages assail us from all sides.

Secondly, people do not make decisions to purchase on straightforward grounds; the process gets muddied by both rational and irrational factors.

> When dealing with people, let us remember we are not dealing with creatures of logic. We are dealing with creatures of emotion, creatures bristling with prejudices and motivated by pride and vanity.
>
> DALE CARNEGIE
> (See Further Reading.)

Suitability for the purpose and how long we think the product will last (the sort of factors we probably *tell* ourselves we rely upon) are not always uppermost in our minds at the time of purchase. We are also influenced by intangibles, such as self-image, dreams and aspirations. The marketer has to understand this complexity and come up with the right message presented in the right way to try to motivate a purchase.

Finally, it is important to recognise that simply communicating the sales message does not ensure purchase. There is very seldom a direct cause and effect route from advertising to sales; in reality it's much more complex. The marketing message must therefore be very flexible; taking the customer through a variety of stages, from total ignorance of a product, through dawning awareness and interest to, we hope, trial and repeat purchase.

The form of the message must also take into account the fact that different people respond at different rates. In his book *The Marketing Plan* Malcolm H. B. McDonald estimates that only 2·5 per cent of the population will buy something new because they like to be different; most people respond much more slowly. And even if your product becomes the market leader, you will have to try to hang on to your market share. Your communication strategy will therefore have to prevent the market becoming bored with the product and at the same time encourage any remaining laggards to consider purchasing it. To achieve this, different techniques must be used at different stages of the campaign – perhaps a poster to shout a message early on, backed up by direct mail at later stages.

It is worth noting that the range of promotional techniques has become much more complex in recent years. Today the producers of mass market products, who at one time would have relied almost exclusively on poster and space advertising, are using highly targeted and personal selling techniques such as direct marketing and sales promotion as part of their range of strategies, mainly to hang on to their brand loyal customers. For example, Heinz announced in Spring 1994 that henceforth they would not advertise individual products but instead the company's brand name, and would use direct mail to promote brand loyalty amongst their customers through special 'club' type promotion e.g. product information and money-off coupon.

This chapter describes all the different methods of getting a sales message across and explains how to concentrate your resources in order to communicate most effectively. The promotional mix can be divided into two overall areas: **impersonal** and **personal** selling methods.

Impersonal promotional methods can be divided up as follows:

- **informational** (such as catalogues, brochures and leaflets)

- **above the line** (paid for, such as space advertising)

- **below the line** (promotions and other negotiated activity)

- **point of sale** (a sales message where goods are sold)

- **free** (such as publicity and public relations)

Personal promotional methods include:

- the use of **sales representatives**

- **direct marketing**

Of course this sort of list is necessarily artificial and there is a lot of blurring at the edges. For example, personal selling relies heavily on informational marketing materials, and direct marketing is often dependent on space advertising to create initial product awareness. But at least a formal list helps us identify what kind of promotional activities we are talking about.

The mix of promotional techniques will vary according to the kind of product/service being promoted. For example, there would be little point in a manufacturer of filing cabinets and office furniture, who promotes almost exclusively by direct mail, employing a PR specialist, except perhaps freelance from time to time, for help on specific projects. A charity or pressure group, on the other hand, will rely heavily on a press officer or publicist to organise free and positive publicity, both for individual projects and for the organisation as a whole.

Likewise, the person responsible for promotion can also vary. The work may be organised in-house, out-house or as a combination of the two. But, whatever means of promotion is used, it should always be financially viable (i.e. designed with specific financial goals in mind; extra sales being the most obvious example).

Informational items

The official face of your organisation

Most organisations have a variety of different, but very standard, pieces of information about themselves that they regularly circulate: their letterhead; business cards; recruitment advertising; panels on the sides of company vehicles and so on.

Do ensure that all these items present an image that is positive, consistent, and takes into account the reader's ability to absorb information about your company. For example, messages on the side of company transport need to be brief, but slightly more detailed information on the company letterhead or in recruitment advertising can be a very successful way of promoting a good image for your organisation.

In-house information

Before considering the variety of different forms your external promotional material may take, it is worth mentioning what gets said about a product in-house, during its development and manufacture.

My main advice to marketing personnel is to involve yourself early. If you don't understand the initial description, or feel it is too wordy or lengthy, attempt to unravel the meaning now rather than just accepting it. Once a difficult set of words have become familiar, everyone will *assume* that they know what they mean. The research and development team who have worked on the product from its earliest days are probably not the best people to explain clearly to the world outside what it is actually for and how it works. If they were they would be in marketing, not in research and development.

The starting point for all copy should be what the customers need to know in order to make a buying decision, not what you might want to tell them about the development process. Use everyday vocabulary and try to avoid technical details; you are not always going to be writing for subject specialists. If there is a lot to say divide it up with subheadings – long dense copy is a distinct turn-off. What is new about it? Who will buy and use it? What needs does it meet? Why did your firm decide to market it? Why should retailers stock it? Why is the product better than the competition?

Such ready-made, working copy, available for adaptation, will be very useful should last-minute marketing ideas come along – for example, space advertisements at a substantial discount just before a journal or magazine goes to press.

Catalogues

Most firms produce a description and stock/price list of their products or services for a wide variety of uses: as reference material for buyers who might try another product; for use by reps and at exhibitions; for PR and so on.

Successful management of the preparation and production of catalogues is very important – not only do they stimulate orders by presenting the firm's wares in an attractive light, they are part of the regular selling cycle which the retail trade is used to responding to and hence expects. Catalogues are also a lasting form of promotion: once the initial ordering has been done, few are thrown away; in retail outlets and on customer's shelves they continue to function as reference material for enquiries and specific requests.

Having said they are necessary, they also tend to be considered rather dull, far less 'creative' than other aspects of marketing. Amassing product information (including all

the last-minute entries that suddenly appear), checking spec-
ification and production details, rounding up illustrations,
dealing with design and production, all involve a tremendous
amount of detailed work.

Getting the catalogues out on time is far more important
than making them totally accurate. Last-minute changes will
always appear; it's more important for the information to
arrive when your customers are expecting it – and when your
competitors will make sure theirs arrive too. Last-minute
news can always be passed on in a press release or provide a
reason for writing to customers about something of interest
to them – a good example of customer care.

How often catalogues are produced depends on the type of
products being promoted. Many firms produce six-monthly
catalogues (usually autumn/winter and spring/summer), or
yearly, to fit in with their marketing and selling cycles, the
catalogue forming the basic document for presentation at the
sales conference that precedes each new selling season.
Other firms send out catalogues more regularly, perhaps
monthly, using the operation as a form of customer service.

The copy contained in a catalogue should vary according
to the anticipated readership and use, with the marketing
department adapting the basic product information as
required. To get ideas on how to present information clearly
and attractively, study both the catalogues of your competitors and those of firms which have nothing to do with your
industry (e.g. consumer goods sold by direct mail). The
following tips will also be useful:

- Make it clear (through space allocation and illustration)
  which are your key products.

- Include at least one order form, preferably several.

- Print your telephone and fax numbers really large to
  encourage your customers to get in touch with you.

- Make the layout user-friendly: use running heads at the
  top of the page (e.g. 'Household Goods' or 'Autumn
  Fashions for Women') to make it clear which section of
  the catalogue you are in; provide a contents list and an

index (both are vital for accessing information in a hurry).

- Highlight what is new (perhaps with a flag sign saying 'new').

- Include as many illustrations as possible to break up the copy and stimulate desire for the products.

For catalogues that will be used in one-to-one selling, for example by a representative, a light-coloured cover allows key notes to be written, and noticed later on by the recipient. For catalogues aimed at specific and perhaps vocational markets, a letter on the inside cover of the catalogue can attract wide attention.

Leaflets and flyers

In general I would count any printed promotional item with a fold or more than two colours as a leaflet, and single sheets as flyers. Flyers are cheaply produced leaflets.

The information you provide will depend on the purpose for which the leaflet/flyer is to be used, but in general try to make the format suit as many possible anticipated needs as you can. You can then add a letter to turn it into a mailshot, enclose it in journals as a loose insert, or send it out with a press release to provide further product information. Give details of how to order. If you are producing a range of flyers on different products for insertion in mailings and handing out at exhibitions, do make them look different. Most people view in a hurry and if they see a format they recognise they assume the information is the same on each and look no further.

Turning one informational item into another

A word processor enables you to be very flexible when preparing promotional material. You can write the basic copy for several different leaflets at the same time, including more features and benefits according to the space available. You can run up cheap and effective flyers in an afternoon;

complete leaflets if you have access to a desktop publishing system. Even without the help of computers, there are a lot of ways to make your budget go further.

For example, if your catalogue is designed as a series of complete pages or double page spreads, could these be turned into leaflets later on? With this in mind, if you are working in more than one colour, ensure that anything you may want to delete (such as page numbers) appears in black only, as this is the cheapest plate for the printers to change. You may also find that your material can be reprinted for subsequent use in two rather than four colours in order to save money.

Likewise, some firms print a new product or stock list in the centre of their regular catalogue, usually on different-coloured paper. If you print extra copies you will find lots of uses for them. As well as providing a useful checklist of products for inclusion in mailings and parcels, they can be handy at exhibitions, or to include with general enquiries/job applications.

Above the line marketing (paid-for promotional items)

Planning space advertisements

When writing advertisement copy, you need to learn how much information to present in the space available. The amount of information you include will depend on:

- how much there is to say about the product

- how much the market needs/wants to know about the product to make a buying decision

- what you are expecting readers to do as a result of seeing your advertisement (Are you just providing product information or expecting orders by return of post?)

For example there is more to say about a new unit trust fund than petrol; more about a new encyclopedia than a novel by a Hollywood film star. The main product benefits, a testimonial from a third party (e.g. a product review or a quotation from a satisfied user), and a guarantee of satisfaction should almost certainly be included. Where there is little to say about a product there is a lot of scope for imagination (as demonstrated by lager advertisements).

Booking advertising space

Standard advertising rates are daunting, so remember that very few people ever pay the full price. Always ask what discounts they offer; sometimes space becomes available at the last minute at a substantial discount. One marketing director I know, who spends a lot of money on taking advertising space in the quality press, always tries out new publications for possible inclusion in her marketing plans on either 'cancellation' or 'trial' rates. Her advice on booking space is 'Don't just disregard the rate card; tear it up!'

Classified ads

Classified advertising is one of the cheapest methods of promotion. You don't even have to pay for typesetting, as it is usually provided by the publication in which it is to appear. Witty contributors to some magazines' classified sections (e.g. *Private Eye*) have ensured they get widely read.

The downside is you have little space, cannot illustrate and there are lots of similar advertisements competing with yours. So, try to use the variables at your disposal to attract attention. For example, experiment with different type densities, capital and lower-case letters. Quote a third-party opinion. Give an incentive to respond immediately, such as ring for a free brochure.

Semi-display ads

Semi-display advertising allows you to use borders, illustrations and other typographic techniques such as reversing out text. Don't take the permission too liberally; if you use too many design techniques your copy will be very hard to read. Do allow plenty of white space around the advertisement – it helps to draw the eye in. Have a look through your local free directories to see how effective – or otherwise – a small advertising space can be.

Advertorials

Advertorials are advertisements that pretend to be editorial copy. In an editorially biased magazine or paper, the advertising guru David Ogilvy reckons six times as many people read the average editorial feature as read the average advertisement. It follows that if you make your advertisement look like editorial copy it will be more widely read. Many of the 'advice' pages in women's magazines today are in fact advertorials, paid for by the manufacturers of the products discussed. You may have to print 'Advertisement' at the top (though don't volunteer to do this unless asked!), and your copy will have to be written in an editorial style, with less puff and more realism. The compensation is that your message will gain in authority and certainly be more widely read. One word of warning: be careful that you don't end up paying for what the magazine would, with a little persuasion, have printed free as a feature.

Television ads

If you are choosing between press and television as the best medium for a campaign, in general the less there is to explain about a product the better suited it is to television. Cheaper products also tend to work better on television. If customers are being asked to spend a lot of money they need a fuller explanation of benefits than is possible during an average length advertisement. An alternative is to give a telephone number for further information at the end of the commercial, a technique that is often used in insurance advertisements or those giving information about government privatisations.

Below the line marketing (promotions)

Below the line marketing is promotional activity for which there is no invoice for space. There is usually an augmented offer to the consumer – more than just the product itself – and a time limit.

For example, a cereal manufacturer might offer advertising space on the back of their cereal packets to a third party selling non-competing goods to a similar market, say a producer of fitness videos. In return, the video manufacturer might provide an incentive for the customer to purchase the cereal – free videos to customers who collect the coupons printed on the back of the packets. The cereal manufacturer hopes the customers will keep buying to collect coupons and videos, and at the same time stockpile the product in their homes and thus become brand-loyal customers. The video producer hopes this greatly increased exposure will increase the demand for their products, and that this will continue once the promotion is over. Most of these deals are coordinated through sales promotion agencies.

When promotional incentives were first widely tried, around 20 years ago, they were seen as short-term buying stimuli, that would only lead to temporary shifts in sales patterns. It was thought that coupons and 'trivial games' would not persuade consumers to change their buying habits permanently. Today such promotions have lost their tacky image. They are now widely regarded as providing the basis for highly targeted marketing campaigns and their long-lasting and very persuasive powers are recognised. Specialist promotion agencies are today securing much of the budgetary spend that traditionally went to advertising agencies.

Promotions can be carried out at different stages of the marketing process, and can be targeted at various groups (stockists, consumers and influencers), with various aims. For example, competitions in which consumers have to absorb product information before entering are a good way of **establishing or changing attitudes**.

Promotions can also **impart information**. For example, a free reader offer at the end of a product news feature in a magazine (such as free samples of the item discussed for the first 100 readers to write in) increases the impact and readership, and prolongs the promotion. Barclaycard, for instance, gave Transworld Publishers a full page of editorial space in their *Perspectives* magazine in exchange for the opportunity of running a feature on Jilly Cooper's novel *Polo* when it first came out.

Other promotions are designed to **encourage repeat purchase**. Free gifts in cereal packets are necessarily cheap, so these are gradually being replaced by coupon schemes whereby points towards a more valuable item are collected. The customer must buy the product several times in order to secure the item, and in return gains a more desirable incentive.

Yet other promotions are aimed at **motivating the sellers**. Competitions for window displays or shifting lots of stock, ready-made attractive display materials, prize draws for something that those who retail your goods want to win can motivate them to shift your product.

For example, in the summer of 1994 Pavilion Publishers announced a cookery promotion with their two lead titles *Ken Hom's Chinese Kitchen* and *Vatch's Thai Cookbook* (by Vatcharin Bhumichitr). They persuaded Thai Airways to give them four free return flights to Thailand, and Dusit Hotels to offer free accommodation in the area. They then announced two competitions: one for the retail trade and a second for consumers. The trade competition was for the best window display of the books (attractive point-of-sale materials were available free of charge in return for a large order of stock). For the consumer competition, organised through bookshops, entrants had to buy the book (or borrow it, thereby resulting in library sales). The result was nationwide window coverage in bookshops and much larger sales than could otherwise have been expected. The costs to the publisher, not counting staff time in pursuing the deals, were minimal in relation to the coverage and sales obtained.

Similarly, sales representatives can be encouraged to put in extra effort if you offer an incentive linked to personal sales results. Telemarketing agencies use a range of promotional techniques to keep their staff motivated such as prize draws and games.

Competition promotions are a good way of **extending your media coverage** without paying for space, as there has to be some basic explanation of the prize (usually the product being promoted). To encourage entrants, try to match the level of the question to the media in which the feature is appearing. For local papers keeping the questions simple will encourage more entrants; tie-breakers tend to put people off.

The list of entrants to a competition will also **provide you with a perfect mailing list**. These people have already absorbed a good deal of product information so, once you have announced the winner, you could consider offering them the chance to buy the product at a special discount instead.

Money-off promotions can be used to **increase customer loyalty** by tempting them to visit a particular store again – hence the popularity of customer loyalty schemes such as the Total Tops scheme, or ASDA Checkout Saver. In the latter scheme customers are provided with a money-off voucher for a subsequent visit based on information provided by them at the checkout (for example, money off children's clothing if they have bought nappies or other children's items).

Money-off vouchers to **encourage the customer to try something new** are an old gambit. Similarly, free samples can generate lots of goodwill and yield important market research information at the same time. The sample of the product should always be accompanied by an incentive to purchase again (such as a money-off coupon).

Point of sale

The point of sale is the place where the customers part with their money in return for the goods. It follows that this is a very good place to remind customers of your product benefits, and many firms produce retail promotional materials for just this purpose.

Writing copy for the package

The most important point-of-sale information is the package. What appears on the outside is very important: it is often the deciding factor in whether or not to buy. If you watch how customers in shops assess products, you will see that the most common sequence is to look at the front of the package and then, if sufficiently interested, turn to the back – or sides – for further information.

Answer all the questions you would want answered by a salesperson, if one were available. The copy should cover all the essential sales points:

- what is new/unique about the product
- what it is for
- who it is for (age group and lifestyle)
- the manufacturer's reputation
- any quotable third party opinions (e.g. extracts from reviews and/or the views of satisfied users or experts)
- brief instructions on how to use it
- the specifications (e.g. quantity/ingredients etc)

The design of the pack should make the brand instantly recognisable; once customers have got used to your brand and decided that they like it, the time taken to select the product will be very short indeed (hence the success of supermarket 'copycat' brands). Make the copy easy to read: don't centre the text or fit it around 'cut out' pictures so that the reader has to work hard to understand it. Keep both sentences and paragraphs short and punchy.

Other point-of-sale materials

Posters, showcards, dumpbins (cardboard display containers to hold the product), till handouts, shelf wobblers and other point-of-sale materials are produced by manufacturers to attract customers' attention in retail outlets. The market's understanding should be instant, so such material should not be too clever or include too much copy. Sometimes such items are not even displayed by the stores who accept them, but serve to demonstrate to the retailer that a manufacturer is highlighting a major product and so form an effective method of ensuring advance orders.

Don't make them too cumbersome, or difficult to put up. Bear in mind that these days many retail outlets spend a lot of money on store design and will not compromise their layout by putting up your aisle-blocking material, however attractively produced.

If you are attempting to get retail outlets with no experience of selling your type of merchandise to stock your goods you will almost certainly have to provide the right housing. For example, many manufacturers have woken up to the fact that garden centres and gift shops in historic buildings are good places to sell consumer goods. In most cases they have had to provide the display cases as well as the products.

'Free' marketing

'Free' marketing is the pursuit of coverage, mostly in the media, without paying for the space or time involved. However if you take into account the salaried hours and expenses spent on pursuing journalists in relation to the coverage actually achieved, most 'free' publicity is anything but free.

News coverage or a feature in an influential newspaper, or important trade journal, or on a widely viewed television programme can make your message reach a much wider audience, offering you the chance to inform public opinion and reorientate popular debate, or simply to spread information about your product by word of mouth. The endorsement of your product by a well-known third party can *really* get your company talked about. For exceptionally hot stories you may even find the media paying for the chance to write about you.

People expect *you* to speak well of your product, whereas review or coverage by an independent third party carries much greater weight. And when media coverage is linked (as it always should be) to information on how to buy or order the product, you should achieve your real aim: larger sales.

But there are risks involved. Not paying for the space taken up means that you sacrifice editorial control over what is said about your product, and that what *is* said, is much more likely to be believed. Was the Hollywood starlet right when she said 'there's no such thing as bad publicity'? Consider what happened when Gerald Ratner grabbed the headlines:

> He implied in April 1991 that consumers were prepared to buy 'total crap'. The company's share price slumped from about £2 to less than 8p in a year. And group profits fell from £112m in 1991 to losses of £122m a year later. (Jon Rees, 'Perils of Changing a Brand Name', *Marketing Week*, 26 August 1994.)

Most techniques for free marketing involve persuading someone that your company/product is worth talking about. With an increasingly hard-nosed press, interested in anything that will boost their circulation or ratings and not in the least constrained by finer feelings or embargoes, there are dangers. They may decide to run a story about how your company does *not* live up to the very promotional claims you wanted them to highlight.

To succeed in this tricky area, you need:

- determination
- persuasiveness
- knowledge of and belief in your products
- imagination, to think up specific opportunities and angles that will appeal to particular media
- a voice and personality that comes over well on the telephone
- a good selection of contacts, built up and carefully maintained
- a good memory
- and, perhaps most important of all, a very thick skin

Building up your links with journalists

Planning press coverage is easiest if you have an existing network of media contacts with whom you are in touch on a regular basis. But this is a hard area to pin down: magazines come and go very quickly today, and even those that survive are seldom static, as the constant wave of relaunches and refocusing on target markets shows. You need to keep track of the changes.

It is a good idea to make a list of all the journals and programmes likely to be significant to your product list and find out the names of the features or news editors. Ring up and introduce yourself; confirm that he or she is the right person to send information to; check the address and the spelling of their name. Ask if you can take the most important contacts out to lunch: it will be easier to sell ideas if your face is already known. Then, armed with your list of contacts, try to feed the right people with the right information at the right time, and in a way that they are most likely to use.

Don't just pursue contacts in the media that you read or

watch yourself. Try to get into the habit of buying a variety of different papers and magazines to see what opportunities for coverage they offer, and watch/listen to broadcast programmes of all kinds. Similarly, don't forget to send copies of your press information to the Press Association (see Useful Addresses) who may feed it to many different international/regional media. Your local papers or radio station may very well do a feature too.

Whatever system you decide on for the management of your lists of contacts, do keep the information on your desk, ready to refer to at all times. I find the best method is a card index. If your lists are manually held, write out each card individually; if your list is managed on computer, produce a set of labels and stick one on each card. Once the system is established, be very methodical about recording ideas that particular contacts have responded well or badly to in the past, their days off, the best times to contact them, and so on. *After each call, note down the reaction to what you offered straight away.* You may think you'll remember, but I find even ten minutes later I can't remember who said what, particularly if I am saying more or less the same thing to each contact!

If you are starting from scratch, a good way to build up press information is either to use directories and year-books (ask in your local library) or to subscribe to the services of a media agency such as PIMS London (see Useful Addresses). For an annual subscription you will receive a manual (and updates) which lists all the press names you might need; you can order them on sticky labels whenever you want to send out a press release.

Achieving good publicity for your company

The usual approach is to send out a press release alerting journalists to some kind of story. You offer the story and the chance for them to feature it, either by arranging an interview or coming along to an event you have organised.

It always pays to follow up a press release with phone calls to those journalists you particularly want to take up the story. Whether or not you get coverage is often due not just to the interesting nature of the story you present but the surrounding package of ideas you offer. You are trying to tempt the journalist to cover your story to the exclusion of all the others competing for his or her attention, so do be imaginative!

Suggest ideas for features that sound appealing – locations, people, animals, vehicles – perhaps in unusual combinations. Remember that features do not have to be written by the paper in question, and you are free to suggest ideas around the subject of your company or product, perhaps from satisfied users or members of staff talking about the human factors associated with a new development.

When is the best time to contact journalists? The best time seems to be after about 10·30am until about 12·45pm; then from about 2·45pm until 4·30pm. It isn't that those are the only times they work, just that those times provide the best chance of catching them at their desks.

Writing an effective press release

The essential function of a press release is to attract attention; to make your story stand out from the crowd and ensure that you get some news or feature coverage. (You should see how many press releases the average journalist receives in one day!)

The first couple of paragraphs should tell the basic story: they should be enticing but short; pithy but stimulating. Whilst making the journalist want to know more, the release should provide sufficiently coherent information for inclusion in the paper should he/she decide to use it straight away. (Sub-editors, especially those on regional papers or local radio, may have gaps to fill and be looking for copy. If your information is succinct and sufficiently interesting, it may get used whole.)

Follow the initial explanation with an expansion of your arguments, illustrated with examples from whatever you are promoting. Never include information in quotation marks: it implies the story has already been covered. Provide relevant information on any associated personalities (e.g. key company personnel or famous users) to prompt the journalist to ask for an interview.

Remember that, as with any other written promotional material, long blocks of copy in a press release put the reader off. Illustrations, particularly cartoons, attract attention. Provide clear information about what the recipient should do next: whom they should ring to arrange interviews; how to obtain samples and so on. And ensure that you have included all the key information, should the release get used whole: availability, price and so on.

Adding an embargo date to the bottom of your release means that every journalist has the same chance to prepare the story before publication; no one *should* print the information before that date. You also risk them putting it to one side and losing it.

Local journalists want very local news. The press release below was used almost whole by the *Folkestone Extra* because although a national story, it was given a Folkestone twist. It was also sent with a very attractive photograph, which, commented Jane Barlow, Reporter on the *Folkestone Extra*, 'virtually guaranteed its inclusion. We are always short of good photographs and welcome them.' The release is written in a chatty style, very appropriate to local papers.

I contacted Christine King, BT Press Relations Manager at Canterbury. Faced with the problem of making a 'dead subject' come alive in a very quick turn-around time (telephone directories are distributed as soon as they come off the press so there is no time for studio shots), she commissioned a photographer to take a shot at their printing site. They came up with an image of a reader supposedly 'quality checking' the printed directories, surrounded by copies of the book and with the cover picture of Canterbury clearly visible. Christine also revealed that her background was in local journalism, hence the easy-to-read style of the release.

BT
CU95042

 *News release*
February 20, 1995

NEW STYLE PHONE BOOK FOR FOLKESTONE

BT customers are discovering that Folkestone's most widely read book has had a face lift.

Delivery of the 246,873 phone books throughout East Kent started this week – enough books end to end to stretch from Canterbury to Gravesend.

Although the cover is still the same, the interior of the BT phone book has been redesigned to make it easier for customers to find the numbers they are looking for.

Major changes include:

- Separate business and residential sections

- Use of the national dialling code instead of the exchange name

- Removal of repeated surnames

Business listings are now contained in their own section in the front of the book.

This change has been made as market research has shown that 70 per cent of numbers looked for in a phone book are those of businesses.

People will no longer have to look up the dialling code when using the phone book – it is included in the entry for the customer in addition to the address.

Another innovation for the new book – and one that customers will take time to get used to – is the removal of repeated surnames. For example Smith is listed just once, with the initials of customers sharing that surname underneath. This cuts down on the amount of paper used, making the book slimmer and more environmentally friendly.

more ...

Shaun Wilson, Phone Book Project Manager, said: 'As part of BT's commitment to putting its customers first, we are always looking at ways of improving our service.

'One request we have responded to in this new book for East Kent is for the national codes to be printed alongside our customers' entries,' he said.

For those customers who are unable to hold, handle or read the phone book BT provides a free Directory Enquiry Service. Details can be obtained by calling free on 195.

One other adjoining phone book, for example Tunbridge Wells or Medway, can be obtained free from BT. To get an additional book residential customers should ring 150 and business customers should call 0800 777 666. Both calls are free.

On the subject of the old phone book don't just throw it away in the dustbin. Take it to a paper bank at one of the local recycling points where they are being collected to be recycled into cardboard.

(ENDS)

Enquiries on this news release should be directed to Christine King, BT Press Relations Manager on Canterbury (01227) 474022.

<u>Remember Phoneday – April 16, 1995 – when all UK national dialling codes will change.</u>

BT and PIPER device is a registered trademark of British Telecommunications Plc.

Making your release personal

Ensure that what you send each journal is relevant. Don't devalue your press releases by producing them too often or sending them to the wrong homes. If you send information 'just in case' to journals you think are not really likely to be interested, they will almost certainly take the same view. The danger is that they may then ignore what you send in future.

Consider making your release specific to a particular journal or broadcasting channel. They all want to scoop their rivals and if you offer a particular opportunity to them alone you may get greater coverage than if the story appeared briefly everywhere at once. For example, when launching a new product, consider offering specific media the chance to interview staff who worked on its development, or who trialled it for you. A classic example of securing coverage in return for an exclusive right to feature is the way publishers sell serial rights for forthcoming newsworthy books. For example, extracts from *Diana, Her True Story*, were first published as a serial in the *Sunday Times*. The newspaper paid for the right to print before anyone else, and the publisher received extra income as well as superb publicity.

If there are very few names on your contact list, tailor what you send to each one. 'Special to ...' at the top of the release may well increase the likelihood of your information being used.

Telephone calls can also help establish how a particular journal wants information presented and suggest the angle from which your product will be looked at. The easier it is for a paper's staff to utilise your information as it stands, the more likely it is to be printed.

Reviews

Product reviews offer the tremendous advantage of a third party opinion at no cost to you, and if that opinion is favourable you are free to quote it as widely as you like. The disadvantage is that you are likely to be compared very closely with your competitors and your product may not perform as well as theirs.

If you have difficulty arranging review coverage in a journal you support through advertising it may be politic to touch *gently* on the relationship between advertising and editorial; in most cases the one pays for the other and it is common practice for the advertising department to sell space around forthcoming editorial features. Editorial independence must be ensured but, as a supporter of the magazine, you have a right to have your products looked at. Undoubtedly the best way is to avoid the issue arising in the first place by making friends with the review editor and keeping in touch about anything you send in.

Interviews on the air

As well as setting up interviews in newspapers and magazines, would your company or product make interesting listening or viewing? Are there specific programmes that might be interested? If the station is not interested in one story, offer a different one and you may still secure coverage ('switch selling'). Don't forget that local radio stations offer lots of opportunities for coverage.

How you prepare for a broadcast interview will depend on the style of the interviewer: whether he or she is likely to be 'hard' (like Jeremy Paxman) or 'soft' (like the majority of local radio interviewers). Politicians react to a hard interviewer by 'springboarding' (using each question as a launchpad to talk about the essential points they wish to get over). The 'hard' interviewer resists tangents and puts forward difficult questions that demand proper answers, not waffle. A 'soft' interviewer will allow the interviewee to be in control of the discussion, guiding or prompting with questions to ensure an interesting programme, or to change the subject (about four minutes per topic is considered sufficient for the attention span of the audience for popular radio).

If you are being interviewed, immerse yourself in all the information you can find and practise answering questions. But you should not over-rehearse; you will sound wooden and unconvincing. Talking from memory (rather than your notes) enables you to give your complete attention to the questions being asked. Whatever you do, don't read out a prepared statement; not only does this sound very impersonal but if the information is already in your press release the interviewer will probably have used it to introduce you. Keep one or two key statistics to hand, but remember that figures are hard to absorb at first hearing. Don't use too many; alternatively, use fractions instead.

Live interviews need not be terrifying; the knowledge that it is for real (not for editing later) can help you to marshal your thoughts. It is easy to forget how many million listeners there are when you are actually talking to just one.

Parties

Parties can generate press interest if the right people are there. Suitable occasions include launches for new products, staff passing professional exams or the handing over of a company donation to charity. Even if you can't get a press photographer along, employ one yourself and then send the results to the right papers. Try offering a picture to one paper as a scoop in return for a guarantee that it will be featured in a prominent place. When circulating a photograph, always stick a good caption on the back: it can make the difference between the shot being featured and being ignored.

Photographs

Newspapers today are much more aware of the value of a good photograph than they used to be. No longer do all images have to appear as illustrations to the text; a good photograph and caption can form a feature on its own. Be imaginative – a row of people lined up with drinks in their hands is very boring.

Exhibitions and trade fairs

Most companies receive regular invitations to exhibit at exhibitions and trade fairs. The outlay can be considerable, with the cost of the stand, the display staging and the loss of key staff members from the office; all hopefully offset by an increase in business. They do provide a good opportunity for networking and making business contacts. Even if leads are not plentiful in supply, your stand price usually includes a list of attendees (useful for cross-checking against your own list of stand callers) plus you have the chance to assess market conditions and see what your competitors are up to. In the case of some exhibitions, where the location is difficult or the timing awkward, it may be worth booking a space just to secure the relevant lists in order to find out who attended (and exhibited).

Press conferences

These should only be called if you have definite news to impart. If you call a press conference and there is no news story you will make journalists wary of accepting your invitation the next time you ask them.

You will need someone to chair the event: to coordinate questions and ensure that all the main points get raised. It could be a key figure in your own company. Alternatively, consider asking someone with related interests who may be a 'name' in his or her own right. If chairing your press conference links them with a cause they support they may do a particularly good job for you.

When deciding when and where to organise, consider the media you most want to cover the event, and what they will find most convenient. Your luxurious offices in the Midlands may not attract many London-based journalists. If you are seeking coverage in the Sunday papers, don't hold your conference too early in the week, and definitely not on a Monday (the day off for most Sunday paper journalists). If you are providing refreshments, make sure they can be consumed quickly and neatly, preferably whilst carrying on a conversation; the most common mistake is not to lay on enough soft drinks. Send out invitations with a press release, but prepare a further sheet with the key details for distribution at the event, which can be taken away by those wanting to write up the story straight away.

Promotional tours

The recording, film and publishing industries use artist/author tours and signing sessions for promotional purposes. For the sufficiently well-known artist, supported by lots of pre-event publicity, this can generate lots of media coverage and accelerate word-of-mouth recommendation of the product and the company behind it. Many writers and recording artists will take stock of their own products to events they attend in case the audience wants to buy.

Stunts

From poetry reading on Waterloo Station, to featuring your promotional message on the side of Battersea Power Station, it's up to you and your imagination. It's worth mentioning that you should make sure that any stunt you arrange *really is* relevant to the main aim of press coverage; i.e. selling more stock. The punters should remember both the event and the product.

Prizes

It's a well-known maxim that people take you at your own estimation; it follows that if you take yourself seriously, so will other people. Do the same for your product. Someone has to win prizes so enter your product or company. The Booker Prize for fiction now has a huge momentum, practically guaranteeing extra sales for titles on the shortlist as well as the eventual winner. The same can happen with other industry-specific competitions such as architectural awards – striving to produce an excellent piece of work within a deadline can bring new motivation to the whole company. Prizes and awards can also be quoted in future publicity.

Public relations

PR can overlap with publicity and promotions; indeed in many companies the PR and publicity functions are combined. PR, however, implies longer-term relationships, rather than one-off publicity campaigns. PR specialists usually try to influence the views others hold about an organisation, rather than generate specific short-term sales.

Very large firms may have their own specialist to liaise with the press on behalf of both the company (corporate identity and policy) as well as individual interests. Alternatively, they may use an external firm or freelance to act on their behalf.

Keeping track of free publicity

Finally, do keep track of any press coverage that appears. Scan the papers you sent your information to, or employ a cuttings agency such as Romeike and Curtice (see Useful Addresses) to do this for you. As well as keeping a general cuttings file, stick a copy of each item of press coverage in the specific product file so it can be incorporated in future publicity and used on the packet of revised and future versions.

Sales representatives

Personal selling involves direct contact with the sales prospect. The sales prospect may be a retail buyer, the end user, or someone who buys on behalf of the end user (as in the case of most items made for children, or bought as presents). This sort of selling is usually done by a sales representative who visits the customer on behalf of the manufacturing/service company.

Sales representatives see themselves as being at the sharp end of any business, because they are in direct touch with the market. To the customers they visit, they *are* the company.

This is a powerful and influential position. They acquire a good deal of sensitive market information in the course of their jobs and have an enormous influence over the short-term future of the company; *they can deliver the budgeted sales figures*.

At the same time they have a great deal of autonomy – it is often difficult to keep track of exactly what they are saying to customers. They also have the power to achieve self-fulfilling prophecies: it is unlikely that any project the sales force had set themselves against would succeed; likewise, a motivated team can work apparent miracles.

There are a number of advantages to using sales reps. Most stem from the fact that the rep can gather direct information from the customer; adapt the sales message according to the customer's situation and needs; and, of course, ask for the order before leaving. For some goods, reps also reduce the costs of distribution by carrying stock with them.

These days, however, many companies are questioning the viability of keeping an expensive team of sales reps on the road. The installation of electronic point of sale (EPOS) in all major retail outlets means that stock is computer-monitored and repeat orders are generated automatically (taking repeat orders was a traditional job for the rep). Likewise, new product information can be sent to the trade through direct marketing, rather than via a personal call.

At the same time improved and vastly cheaper computers have led to more central coordination and less autonomy for individual store managers. Today the retailer's head office can buy direct from the manufacturer's head office, and order for all its branches at the same time. Because the order sizes are larger, the retail discounts are larger too. Smaller firms tend to buy from wholesalers or respond to telesales operations which, if handled well, can be just as personal as a rep's call, but a lot quicker.

Large companies with multiple branches (such as off-licences) coordinate buying and have stocks delivered to a central warehouse. Individual shop managers then phone, fax or electronically order each week to say how much they want of each standard item; they do not see reps. Similarly, small independent retailers, such as garden centres or do-it-yourself and hardware shops, fax or ring their orders through to wholesalers or large manufacturers on freephone numbers and see reps only for new product information or to discuss special promotions.

Many manufacturers are also approaching their customers directly. Vastly improved analysis systems enable them to identify specific markets and target them, thus cutting out the retailers and their margin. Similarly, the introduction of sophisticated in-house reporting systems can reveal just how profitable each rep's call has (or has not) been.

Nevertheless, even if no longer so widely used as order-takers, reps often continue to visit. Sometimes they work as merchandisers, checking stocking levels of key products. They often collaborate with head office staff in the organisation of local promotions, and they have an important part to play in spreading information about new products and in corporate PR. Similarly, they can be involved in market research, securing local sales and setting up exhibitions.

If you do decide to have a rep force it is vital to ensure three things. Firstly, the goals they strive for should be set by the marketing staff according to long-term plans to penetrate specific market sectors. They should not be short-term goals based on what the sales department already knows from experience is achievable. There is a world of difference between shifting stock to retail buyers who may/or may not do anything with it, and persuading them to meet anticipated demand from the end consumer by actively pushing a product.

Secondly, any information that they pick up in the course of their work must be fed back into the company. And thirdly, they must be kept motivated. For the vast majority of people this means being made to feel valued, secure and involved, not just financially rewarded.

Direct marketing

Direct marketing used to be considered a very impersonal medium – hence the disparaging phrase 'junk mail'. Today it is widely seen as just the opposite, offering the chance to target a marketing campaign at a specific market segment at the time of your choosing, and with a highly personal and carefully tailored message. Direct marketing campaigns are becoming more and more focused; over half the mail is now sent to someone with whom the mailer has dealt before. Telemarketing and party plan selling can also be very targeted and highly personal. This is an important and fast-developing area, worth a chapter on its own (see Chapter 8).

SUMMARY

This chapter has covered the wide variety of promotional techniques that can be used to market a product or service. Whether these techniques are adopted singly or in combination, the aim should be to make it as convenient as possible for customers to gather information, receive a sales approach and buy the product.

5

Production and Distribution

IT'S VERY EASY to get enthusiastic about marketing. Market research can be fascinating; planning advertising is exciting; commissioning design feels creative; tracking the orders that result from direct marketing is nerve-racking but exhilarating. This chapter will deal with aspects of the business that have a less compelling image but are nevertheless vital to effective marketing.

Searching for widgets of a specific size, that are strong enough for the job and get delivered on time, sounds much less glamorous. Managing a warehouse and scheduling delivery lorries so that items can be stored in a logical order can seem equally lacking in glory. To make things worse, the staff involved in these areas are often geographically distant from head office; they are frequently made to feel, or just do feel, alienated from the 'real' business; their lead times tend to be forgotten or put under immense pressure to meet externally (and often artificially) imposed deadlines.

Well, unglamorous they may be, but production and distribution are fundamental elements of marketing. Both are central to the **marketing mix** discussed in Chapter 1 – production to 'product' and distribution to 'place'. And both are fundamental to the success of any company that wants to compete on quality, pricing and availability.

If the production of an item is flawed in design or execution, it doesn't matter how good the advertising is, the whole project will fail. Few people buy for a second time a product or service whose quality they have been disappointed in, a factor that probably accounts for the very high failure rate amongst new restaurants. Reports after disasters sometimes centre on relatively straightforward production problems. Think of the 1986 Challenger space shuttle disaster; the enquiry centred early on a single faulty production component – ineffective 'O' rings. The same goes for distribution. There is little point in producing goods and stimulating demand if they are not in the shops when customers want to buy them.

Production and distribution may have been viewed rather simplistically in the past. But today companies are realising that mastery of these areas offers them a major competitive advantage, a vital factor in difficult trading conditions.

The scope and complexity of the considerations involved has been reflected in the rapid development of the study of logistics, defined by the Institute of Logistics as the 'time related positioning of resources'. There is no area of a business that is unaffected by logistics: from relationships with suppliers to the quality of the product; from the physical distribution of goods to ensuring customer satisfaction. The application of logistics is essential to efficient management of the supply chain. The diagram on page 87 reveals its scope.

I am going to concentrate in this chapter on two key elements of logistics: production and distribution.

Production

A firm's production staff are involved in producing the products. Obviously. However it is rarely as simple as it sounds.

Production can involve many different tasks, such as: sourcing and buying ready-made finished items and 'badging' them for the purchaser (for example, putting the brand name on a pre-made computer); buying externally produced ready-made component parts; or commissioning dedicated items, whether in- or out-house. The production

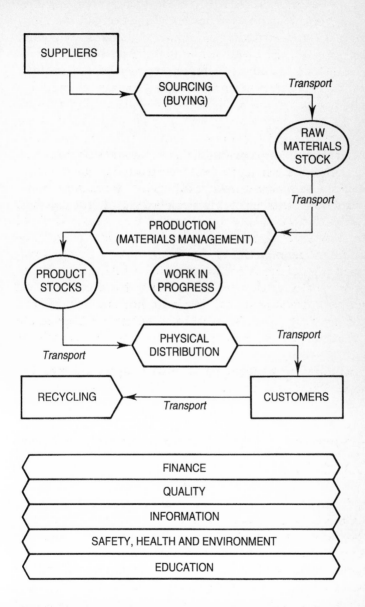

Source: Institute of Logistics

manager has to keep track of different product lines, the quality promised by suppliers, the quantity required, and the deadlines by which they are needed. Lines of communication may become extremely complicated if items are being sourced or produced in other countries. And bear in mind that research and product planning are carried out against the background of a constantly changing market.

Where to produce

The need to maximise profits means that most companies want to achieve a particular level of quality for their goods and services, but at the lowest possible cost. Where to organise production can seem fairly straightforward. Ideally you need:

- a source of raw material
- a source of power
- a means of transporting the goods to the market
- a source of labour
- a market nearby
- a centre of commerce nearby
- a centre of government nearby
- a suitable climate
- a stable political atmosphere

The relative importance of these factors varies according to the kinds of goods and services being produced. If your goods are marketable nationally, where you produce them will probably depend on how easily and cheaply the goods can be transported. Natural resources can often be transported (depending on weight) and locations can acquire advantages in the form of locally available services which have nothing to do with raw materials. Government involvement can also make particular areas very attractive through investment grants and tax concessions to those working there.

How to achieve cost-effective production

Production costs should not be seen in isolation. The production method decided upon can have a fundamental impact on the profit margin, price, quality, styling, timing and longevity of the product.

There are many important questions to be considered. Would a larger order make the product cheaper per unit? Is it more cost-effective to produce another 1000 whilst the production lines are running? What is the most cost-effective number to produce? (Some raw materials are sold in specific unit quantities and ordering slightly less or more will disproportionately increase your production costs.)

Will producing too many varieties make the unit price too expensive? Would slightly reducing the quality of the components have only a marginal effect on eventual quality but make the economics of the whole project work better?

When do you want the raw materials/component parts produced by? (In general the faster you want them, the more it will cost, unless you are in a strong negotiating position.) How quickly must your final product be available? Will insisting on a very rapid turnaround reduce the quality of your goods, thereby eventually costing you more through increased warranty expense, additional preparation changes, lost sales and consumer goodwill?

How are the competition handling production? What are they charging? How much are they paying for production? What is the balance between **price volume** (the volume sold at a particular price) and profit. (Calculating the break-even point will show you how many units you have to sell to recoup your initial production costs, and thus help you estimate the level of risk.)

In my experience good production managers are some of the most dependable of staff. They are usually calm and well organised, with a very good eye for detail. Nothing fazes them. If one supplier lets them down they have several others up their sleeve. What they need from you is advance information on what you want to produce and when. If properly consulted, they will find a way to meet a demanding production schedule.

Having a knowledge of how production teams work can be a great asset. Senior managers who demonstrate that they understand the production implications of what they are asking for, can attract tremendous loyalty from those on the shopfloor.

Distribution

Distribution refers to the physical movement of goods to the point of eventual sale. The type of distribution, and the one I'm going to concentrate on in this chapter, is getting the product or service to the designated market so that customers can buy it. There are other kinds of distribution too, for example the movement of raw materials from producer to manufacturer and the internal distribution systems that most organisations have for relevant information.

Contrary to popular belief, distribution is not just about fixing terms of trade between the manufacturer and the retailer according to the amount purchased; or about counting the days from receipt of order to delivery of product. The reality is both more complex and significant.

Let's start by examining the scale. This is a vast and expensive area, requiring significant investment in property, computerisation and material-handling systems, whether set up in-house or provided by a third party. The scope of distribution today is widening, as more and more companies realise its significance as a marketing asset rather than simply a cost burden.

Distribution is an area of very strong expertise in Britain; we probably offer the most sophisticated service in the world. Lacking an extensive manufacturing base of our own, there has been a strong emergence of companies providing the kind of service that adds value to the firms for whom they work. It has been estimated that distribution already involves around 15 per cent of the UK workforce.

The improvement in efficiency in recent years has been remarkable. For example, in 1980 in Britain it was estimated that distribution costs, as a proportion of sales, were around 17 per cent. By 1992 this had been reduced to 5 per cent, with further reductions likely in the future. Reasons for this fall include more efficient handling of stock, improved transportation and warehousing, more sophisticated computer control systems, and increasing use of **unitised handling** (whereby products are packed in pallets or boxes instead of being sent out as individual items; orders are consequently larger and there is less damage). All these creative strategies are at the disposal of the distribution department. Their cumulative effects are reduced overheads, improved margins and increased profitability.

Distribution also has an important role to play in customer satisfaction. In difficult trading times most companies recognise the importance of customer service in obtaining repeat business. In providing a service, the distributor must ensure the customer's satisfaction at the point and time of delivery. It follows that offering an efficient, reliable and courteous service at the lowest possible cost will have a substantial effect on sales and the amount of profit resulting from each sale. This is an area of substantial investment for many firms at the moment, as they attempt to ensure that they pay sufficient attention to detail to keep the customer satisfied and ordering.

One business sector that is investing heavily in customer care at the moment is the direct marketing industry, selling a variety of goods straight to the customer, usually through mailshots and catalogues. Firms that have tracked ordering patterns have found that complainers who are well handled become loyal customers, subsequently ordering more often than those who have never complained at all!

Planning distribution

Whether you are planning to organise all your distribution yourself or buy a service in from a third party, your distribution plan needs to be aimed at meeting the expectations of your diverse customers. As with all aspects of marketing, you should start with a proper assessment of what you are trying to achieve. Ask yourself the following questions:

- Where are your customers?
- How can you reach them efficiently?
- What level of service do they need (e.g. how fast, how often)?
- What are your main aims? (Initial market penetration, increased market share, or gaining market information in order to sell direct in future?)
- How many outlets are you trying to cover?
- Where are they?
- When do they need the stock?
- How much of your product list do you want to push?
- What customer development programmes do you have? (Future products and services?)

Malcolm H. B. McDonald, author of *The Marketing Plan*, came up with a useful three-part formula for considering distribution: physical distribution, marketing channels and customer service. I'll deal with each one in turn.

Physical distribution

This involves the physical storage and movement of the goods to be sold. Here you need to consider internal and external factors and their associated costs.

Let's begin with storage. Where are the goods to be stored, now and in the future? Will you have individual or cooperative warehousing arrangements? Are the facilities suitable for their purpose? Consider security, durability, insurance, legal restrictions, proximity to major markets, and so on.

How often will you deliver your goods? Industrial buyers accept that the shorter the lead time, the more you pay for the product. It is also standard practice for the length of delivery time to be established when the order is placed, and then built in to the timing of the job. Carriage is normally the responsibility of the supplier, and can be upgraded to faster means if the goods are very urgently required (most suppliers charge freight separately, according to means of delivery). For example, courier delivery would obviously be more expensive than parcel post or rail delivery.

Many firms offer different distribution packages, depending on need (e.g. 'carriage free' or 'carriage paid'; a 48-hour guaranteed delivery at x per cent discount; or seven-day delivery at x+y per cent discount). Offering the customer the choice should make them distinguish between rush and routine orders, balancing speed and cost with level of service required. Instant turnaround is expensive, and perhaps unprofitable, but you may need to offer express delivery at certain times of the year (e.g. pre-Christmas), perhaps in return for a lower discount.

You also need to consider whether there is a seasonal pattern to your company's sales. When are you likely to be busiest?

What kind of transport will you use? Your own or a third party's? If you decide on your own, will you buy the vehicle/s outright, lease or rent?

How will you protect the goods while they are in transit? Damaged, badly packed stock is a cost to your business and will inconvenience your customers.

How will you manage your stock to ensure that orders are fulfilled accurately (e.g. checking that all necessary components are available, that deliveries match expectations in quality, quantity and timing; monitoring shrinkage and product deterioration)?

As far as your own production is concerned, you need to keep your company supplied with any vital materials but carry the minimum of stock, in order to avoid tying up large amounts of cash. For very small, inexpensive items, it is often not worth keeping stock in-house, as the cost of keeping and counting them will outweigh their usefulness or value.

What units will you send the product out in (e.g. most packaged foods go out in an 'outer' pack which cannot be broken up)? What is the balance between product price and distribution costs? If product prices are low and distribution costs high (e.g. for cheap heavy items such as bricks or books), can you supply in certain minimum quantities?

What will your minimum order size be? Are there to be small-order surcharges through add-on charges or reduced discounts? Work out what it costs to retrieve the minimum order size from your warehouse and at what price a consignment starts to make a profit.

What trade discounts will you give? Discounts usually increase in return for the amount of stock held (and hence the amount of risk taken), the speed at which the stock is required and the method of delivery. It's important to relate costs closely to sales revenue.

Who will manage the warehouse staff? Running a warehouse and distribution system can involve complex labour relations issues such as wage negotiations and technical breakdowns.

What quality control systems will you have to eradicate picking errors, shortages and damage? Random checks on accuracy are probably the best way of monitoring, although weight checks are being increasingly used by automated warehouses.

Where will your customer service be handled, and at what level of service will it operate? Can the organisation handling your storage offer this too, and if so at what cost? Who will ensure proper credit management to chase unpaid invoices, and minimise credit risk and bad debts? What will your payment period be?

How will your distribution base and head office communicate? It is common for people to complain that sales and credit management teams do not talk to each other; that information about special discounts or extended credit periods is not passed on. Similarly, it's vital to improve the liaison between marketing and distribution departments, to ensure that the latter understands what variables the former is offering, when and to whom.

Precise data control systems linking sales location and distribution centre minimise in-house service times. This is particularly important when the distances involved are very great, and the penalties for error consequently much increased. If stock is being sold to New York, invoiced in US dollars, and delivered from the UK, it is vital to ensure accuracy.

Improved standards of accuracy are very important for the future too; many firms are already using the latest computer technology and electronic data interchange to support fully automated warehouse systems.

As a practical example of this, Britvic's National Distribution Centre at Lutterworth (operated by Wincanton Distribution Ltd) is one of the most automated warehouses in Europe, designed to meet customer needs to the year 2000. Here the most up-to-date technology has been installed, with automated handling and integral computer systems. Efficiency, unit costs and response times have all improved as a direct result of the new system; all fulfilling the key objective of providing a better service to customers.

There will be an increasing move to electronic ordering (in some cases directly triggering production) and invoicing; the automation of many warehouse functions and wide application of machine-readable codes, at warehouses and point of sale; all providing valuable and easily accessible information to those planning future marketing campaigns.

There are also a number of external factors to consider when planning your distribution. For example, what are the markets for your goods like now and how will they change in the future? Are there any government, legal or ethical restrictions on how the type of goods you produce or sell can be stored or transported? For example, is storage forbidden in your lease or mortgage? Is the media interested in what you do and how? Could your methods of distribution or storage attract adverse publicity (e.g. transportation of live animals)?

What is the competition offering? Does your product have superior market attractiveness? Or do you need to exceed their availability to sustain demand, even if you cannot match what they offer? What marketing channels are available (retailers, wholesalers, agents and so on)?

Having considered all these areas, here are a few guidelines for managing the physical distribution of goods:

1 *Keep it simple*. The more times a product gets handled, the more likely it is to get damaged or lost.

2 *Speed is of less importance than reliability*. Establishing a delivery period is important, but don't always assume the shorter the better; reliability is even more important. A supplier who promises two days and provides a service that varies between one and seven days is less reliable than a client who promises four days and always delivers on time. Your customers will respond in the same way, so bear in mind that key delivery points (such as weekend to weekend) are as sensitive as key pricing points.

3 *Get access to the key information acquired by your distributor*. Whether in- or out-house, your distributor handles all the key information relating to your customers: data on customer ordering patterns; product performance over time; what you can and cannot supply; what gets returned by customers and why; what products you should produce more of and by when. Make sure you have intelligent access to this information, preferably partly digested through computer reports. This should help you identify market patterns and predict which way the market is moving.

4 *Watch out for marketing opportunities through improving distribution*. Those who deliver your goods offer you other opportunities for satisfying your customers. At the same time as they deliver they can, for example, also sell new products, distribute promotional material and collect cash. Don't just concentrate on delivery to the exclusion of other opportunities for marketing contact.

Choosing your marketing channels

You have three basic options: selling direct; selling through intermediaries (e.g. shops or agents); or selling through wholesalers.

Selling direct means that every single aspect of the marketing, from production to delivery and customer service, will be under your control. It's an expensive system to set up, but the resulting profit need not be shared with anyone else. Direct selling usually works best for higher price products, for which there is a specialist market and for which contact lists exist or can be profitably built. (For more on direct marketing, see Chapter 8.)

Selling through intermediaries means that retail or other outlets take stock of your product at a discount and sell at a higher price. Manufacturers need to decide what kind of outlets they will sell their products through. Should the product be widely available or very exclusive? The choice of which intermediaries you sell through is very important; your customers will see the outlets you choose as representing your company.

In most industries the manufacturer provides a recommended retail price (**rrp**) but the actual selling price is set by the retailer. If the retailer wishes, he or she can undercut the competition, thus securing a competitive advantage. Manufacturers who do not wish to see their product sold below the rrp have the option of discontinuing supply to outlets who want to price-cut.

Once an order for stock has been placed, it is the retailer's responsibility to sell it, even if the only eventual option is selling at a reduced price in order to shift what remains. There are certain types of goods (e.g. books, magazines, paint and seeds) which are sold on a **sale or return basis**, meaning that they may be returned to the manufacturer if they do not sell. The same rule applies when new merchandise, or stock of which a store has no previous experience, is on offer. It is standard practice in supermarkets for new stock to be supplied on the basis of 'uplift' if it does not sell. Smaller independent stores, such as hardware shops or wine merchants, are occasionally offered promotional displays, for which the accompanying stock is available on sale or return.

In some markets (e.g. export markets where communications with head office are necessarily weaker) companies may decide to appoint an additional intermediary, such as an agent, to represent their interests. The agent can then deal with local shops. Some firms open up overseas offices in particularly important markets to monitor their local interests themselves.

Selling through wholesalers means that the wholesalers take large quantities of a limited range of stock in order to supply goods to retail outlets. Some wholesalers specialise in certain market areas, e.g. foodstuffs or electrical goods; others deal in a wider variety of goods. They ask for larger discounts than those generally available to retailers because order quantities are high and they are selling on at a discount on rrp themselves. They are also absorbing some of the cost of storage from both producer and retailer. Wholesalers offer retailers the advantage of being able to order a variety of goods from one stocking point, with one delivery time, from one address, and usually very quick delivery.

However their market share has been threatened of late by the growth of very large stores who negotiate directly with producers to obtain larger discounts. The producers too want more control over the supply and more emphatic display of their branded goods and welcome direct contact with large retailers. Similarly, improved transport facilities have threatened the specialised functions of the wholesaler.

A final possible option is the organisation of **collective distribution arrangements**. Single, industry-owned distribution centres, with perhaps just one or two warehouses, are a feature in certain industries. For example, in Britain the various national and (where appropriate) local newspapers are delivered daily to a number of regional warehouses. This results in just one invoice per publication; the whole print run is distributed immediately; and the vast bulk of payment is received within two months of publication.

Which distribution channel you choose will depend on a number of factors:

- the nature of the customer base (how easy they are to reach and how they like to buy)

- the type of product (for example, it would not be cost-effective to sell very cheap goods to the customer direct unless the quantities were very large)

- the resources of the company (what you can afford)

- what other options you have for getting the product to the consumer (e.g. door-to-door sales, party plan, and so on)

Customer service

As we saw in Chapter 1, marketing means getting the right goods to the right customer at the right time, in the right way, at the right price. Achieving this is customer service. The quality of service is generally a sign of business success: 'great products deserve great service' is a popular maxim.

Most companies, whether manufacturers or retailers, have long had a customer service department to handle the service provided to the customer from the time an order is placed until the product is delivered and the customer is satisfied. They usually spend most of their time sorting out problems with individual customers. These problems may be due to dissatisfaction with the product received, or perhaps limited product availability. It will almost certainly be too expensive to offer 100 per cent availability on every product to every potential customer, so a central ordering facility, or information on local availability through customer service departments, can be very useful.

As markets mature, or get more difficult through recession, the quality of the relationship between the producer/retailer and the customer becomes more and more important. Companies that offer a high standard of customer care can often expect long-term rewards of loyalty and repeat business.

In the extremely competitive world of estate agency it has become common public knowledge that many of the corporately-owned chains of estate agents have succeeded in compounding year-on-year losses running to tens of millions of pounds. This is despite the very high profile of the corporate parent companies (e.g. Prudential, Nationwide and Abbey National), widespread advertising campaigns and first-class positioning of premises. Meanwhile, smaller independent firms have succeeded in staying afloat and have even become profitable enterprises in very difficult market conditions. One firm, Penyards, based in Hampshire and Wiltshire, has continued to expand through the recession by providing a very high standard of customer care and therein a steady level of recommended and return business.

The customer reaps similar benefits through actual or impending competition: improved customer service is often the result. For example, the cross-Channel ferry companies have improved dramatically of late in response to competition from the Channel Tunnel. Likewise, telephone companies are providing a better – and cheaper – service now that they have competition.

In many companies these concerns have been developed into a customer care programme, which attempts to nurture the relationship between the supplier and the customer in order to maintain and increase future market share. This means far more than just being nice to customers. Companies who try to better their performance in this way can measure the improvement in service and usually see direct benefits as a result.

These companies can chart how they meet changing customer expectations and how they compare both with the performance of their direct competitors and the service performance of other industries. ITPS (a distribution centre for the publishing industry), for example, found that implementing a customer care programme resulted in much speedier cash collection (satisfied customers pay their bills quickly).

For firms supplying goods or services business-to-business, improving customer care can cement a trading relationship in a way that the sales department alone would find impossible. For example, if queries and problems are swiftly resolved and staff at *all* levels of seniority have a good working relationship, both parties benefit from the increased security of their trading relationship. Competitors will find such a relationship very hard to challenge.

Performance is often tracked by means of surveys. For example, at ITPS there has been extensive monitoring of customer service, through telephone surveys. Regular meetings have been organised with small groups of retailers and 20,000 random trade and individual customers have been surveyed each year on the service they have received. Often customers say how surprised they are when reports of indifferent or poor performance are quickly followed up and amends made. This can lead to practical improvements, such as invoicing German customers in Deutschmarks, employing fluent French speakers to deal with French customers, and having a proper understanding of local needs. Inviting retail customers to visit your offices, and training your staff to be aware of the problems and priorities of your customers can be equally beneficial.

Such programmes recognise the importance of matching service levels to different market segments: not all customers want or expect the same things. For example, in the current battle for market share between UK supermarket chains, ASDA have made providing crèches for shoppers' children a priority, a facility that other chains, according to *Marketing Week*, 'do not even have on the agenda'. Other stores emphasise different benefits: the wide range of goods they stock; the freshness of their produce; the value their own-brand products provide; the help they offer with packing and carrying the goods to the customer's car.

All customer care programmes need to relate the cost of the service they provide to the existing and possible future value of their business relationship with the customer. There is a point where the costs of customer service equal the extra revenue. If the price of the goods on sale is sufficiently high, it may be worth paying for even higher levels of customer service. For example, car manufacturers often provide valuable customer care schemes, with attractive benefits, to keep customers loyal to their brand.

SUMMARY

Production and distribution are fundamental and complex elements of marketing. Properly managed, they should be designed to provide the customer with excellent quality, pricing and availability. Customers whose needs are met are likely to order again, and this is the key to long-term commercial success.

6

Employing External Marketing Services

IF THE MAIN AIM of marketing is to identify and satisfy the needs of your customers, it follows that contacting them, telling them about your products, and creating a sufficiently powerful relationship between them and your product to motivate a purchase, is extremely important. Yet most of the world's largest companies rely on a third party to carry out the vital task of presenting, explaining and conveying this message. Why do they entrust such an important part of the business to outsiders? Why not do it themselves?

Probably because, in most companies, strategies and objectives are provided by internal management but image-making and communications are specialist skills that are best bought in from *objective* outsiders. And good advertising is not as simple as good campaigns make it look.

> Commonsense could help you produce an ad that came close to being fail-proof, if not totally foolproof. The 'rules' would help you avoid error. It still took a little thing called 'talent' to bring the rules to life.
>
> BARRY DAY
> (See Further Reading.)

Professional marketing agencies specialise in keeping up-to-date with trends in society and the media; they know how to influence people and keep a sharp eye on what is working.

They would claim that creative talent is more likely to thrive in such agencies, where individuals working on a variety of different projects can inspire each other, rather than in the manufacturing companies that produced the products in the first place.

On important issues of law or finance, as well as consulting their in-house specialists, most firms rely heavily on an external expert's view. But, although marketing agencies supply a service to firms (in the same way as legal and financial advisers), there tends to be a much closer association with a firm's marketing advisers than with other services employed, most of whom deal with external aspects of the business.

To help a client company communicate effectively, the agency must immerse itself in the company's culture, attitudes and body language. There must be a clear understanding of what the company is good and bad at (i.e. its **competitive differentials**). This is highly sensitive and confidential information. It is therefore a common condition that the agency handles no other directly competing accounts.

How have marketing services changed?

The range and variety of marketing service companies has increased enormously in recent years. Twenty years ago most of the marketing spend consisted of 'above the line' (paid-for) space advertising handled by large advertising agencies. The accepted view was that 'below the line' marketing activity (such as promotions that made use of negotiated rather than paid-for advertising space) might encourage consumers to try a product, but it was the sustained paid-for advertising campaigns that really changed consumer buying patterns and supported brand images over the long term. There *were* some very good long-running promotions (e.g. Robertson's Golly and cigarette cards) but David Ogilvy's view, expressed in 1955, was common: 'Deals don't build the kind of indestructible image which is the only thing that can make your brand part of the fabric of life.'

What is more, most of the advertisers liked to use large agencies. When considering which agency to use, it was very reassuring to see the professional campaigns they had created for other clients. But the large agencies who got most of the business were also very expensive to run; and they became even more so, as new marketing developments encouraged them to take on yet more staff to meet new needs. For example, most of the large agencies added 'direct' operations, as direct marketing took off in the early 1980s. But the extra overheads incurred were seldom matched by a compensating rise in business.

At the same time, over the past few years there has been a decline in the amount of money most firms have been allocating to straight space advertising; clients have begun to want to experiment with different marketing techniques, and the funding usually comes out of the existing advertising budget. Promotional firms have shown that their campaigns are not as 'flash in the pan' as was once thought; they have become much more sophisticated and sustained, and very much a part of the standard armoury of promotion. Some clients have started to employ a second agency to handle direct marketing or promotional work, further increasing the pressure on the large advertising agencies who have to be seen to provide extra value for money in return for their slice of the marketing spend. Some have not survived the challenge.

Today the distinction between above and below the line is no longer so clear-cut; many firms now settle for a combination of different marketing techniques both above and below the line, working in combination, handled by a variety of different operations. Indeed, some marketing service firms have responded to this and are now offering their clients both types of service.

Other reasons for the growing acceptability of a greater

variety of marketing services are not hard to find. Most advertising agencies offer mass marketing, using mass communications channels – television, newspaper display advertising and posters. But society today demands more selectivity and choice; we want to interact, not just absorb. These issues are frequently discussed in the educational press: our attention span has gone down; we walk away if we are not interested; we 'zap' during commercial breaks on television, and 'information snack' from a huge variety of different sources. My father read the *Observer* throughout his life and knew that if any interesting statistic came into his head, it was most likely to be from that source. Today's population is vastly more promiscuous in its information-gathering habits; we have experienced an explosion of customer choice **media fragmentation**.

From the advertiser's point of view, this makes us much less predictable. If market research has revealed that a particular market segment is likely to be watching television at a specific time of night, no advertiser can guarantee any longer that the majority of that market will be watching a channel with commercial breaks; there are too many other options. Even if they do have the television on, the potential customer may be watching a rented video, be tuned in to a satellite channel, be using the remote control to switch to another channel during every advertising break, or be recording the film for viewing later (perhaps using a machine now available that will automatically exclude the commercials from the recording they later see).

Potential advertisers have two main options. They can either widen the range of mass media being used to reach the potential market, to ensure that a greater degree of cover is achieved; or alternatively, they can use the growing selectivity of the population to their advantage. Increased choice makes us much easier to define, and this is where many of the new marketing service companies have succeeded; they offer experience in targeting a message to a specific market sector, emphasising in the process their strategic thinking and analytical abilities rather than just their ability to produce appealing creative work.

The wider use of direct marketing and its very quantifiable feedback have led to a greater desire for accountability in other aspects of marketing. Client companies are now determined to coordinate a whole range of purchased services to ensure that they get value for money. Traditional advertising wisdom accepted that if the product was bad, aggressive advertising would only accelerate its eventual demise. Today, many of the services on offer are to do with enhancing the product and its presentation (for example, changing the name, package and so on to increase its chances of success).

Lastly, the very large agencies made it difficult for the 'creatives' to have much contact with the client; discussions were often handled by account managers who explained the campaign to the client and handled feedback. Distortions and misunderstandings were almost inevitable, and creativity got fogged by too many layers of administration. As discussed in Chapter 1, marketing people are ideas people, who spark in contact and find nothing more ego-boosting than having their advice taken. The past few years have seen a move by talented people in larger agencies to set up smaller, more entrepreneurial enterprises that offer a far greater degree of client contact, and hence mutual satisfaction.

What marketing services are on offer?

Market research

You can commission market research about any aspect of your business, from what kind of people make up your market and what else they buy, to how best to reach them with your promotional message. (For further advice, see Chapter 2.)

Advertising agencies

The advertising agency is perhaps the most familiar marketing service. We have become so used to seeing advertising messages as part of our everyday lives, on television and in the street, that they are sometimes more conspicuous by their absence – as in the former Communist Bloc countries where streets and railway stations, denied their splash of advertising colour, looked extremely drab.

Advertising agencies excel at conveying messages which explain basic product benefits to consumers in order to promote sales. Today many of the larger agencies own other marketing service companies, designed to provide clients with complete management of their commercial communications: advertising, public relations, design, sales promotion, direct marketing, and so on. Most of the largest agencies are international, with semi-independent branches around the world managed by nationals in each country to serve a huge variety of local markets.

This diversification is very important. With the explosion of different media available to advertisers today, and more coming soon (video on demand, interactive newspapers, niche cable TV channels, more information being circulated by PCs and CD-ROM, and so on), agencies must offer advice on communications as a whole rather than conventional advertising techniques. Nevertheless, many have stuck to a rather formulaic approach, ignoring new media opportunities. According to Steven Carter, Managing Director of J. Walter Thompson, 'The last real major innovation was the 30-second TV commercial in 1956.'

Advertising agencies secure business by providing information on themselves and the accounts they have previously worked on ('presenting their credentials') and, if this looks promising, 'pitching for the account', usually in competition with other agencies. The service they offer can either be on a 'full' basis (they create the whole campaign) or 'media only' basis (the agency books the advertising space at a discount, passing back some of the savings made to the client, who produces his own advertisements). For the vast majority of clients who opt for the full service, the subsequent creative campaign will be rooted in a well-developed understanding of their needs, as the agency attempts to build, position and manage the customer's brand assets.

It's a fascinating world, and a good way of keeping up-to-date with what is going on is to subscribe to a marketing magazine. In *Marketing Week* or *Campaign* you can read, week by week, about who is working for whom, how, and with what success. The Incorporated Society of British Advertisers (see Useful Addresses) offers professional advice on dealing with advertising agencies.

Promotion agencies

This has been the most spectacular area of growth in marketing services over the past few years. Promotional activities ('below the line' marketing) promise some additional temporary benefit over and above the basic, and long-term, brand proposition. What usually happens is that two (or more) distinct, and non-competing products, that nevertheless appeal to the same market, are linked in a promotional deal.

For example, a cereal manufacturer might be willing to offer space on the back of the packet in return for an association with the latest 'craze' toys popular with young children. They reason that the link will encourage children to spot the packet, and hence parents to buy the product. They will advertise the link on television, usually offering a free item in return for a number of tokens or proofs of purchase clipped from the carton – thus encouraging repeat purchase by the consumer and stockpiling at home, intended to breed brand loyalty. Both companies expect to benefit from a measurable increase in business.

Most of these deals are arranged by promotion agencies. What is more, a number of manufacturers have cottoned on to the idea of offering their own products as possible promotional incentives, and there are trade fairs and catalogues where they can display their wares.

The downside to promotional deals is that this sort of advertising may be an admission that the product performance and brand image of each product individually is not sufficiently compelling to motivate purchase. Is the promotion securing short-term sales volume at the expense of long-term brand building?

To locate promotion agencies and find out more about below the line marketing, contact the organisations listed under 'Sales Promotion' in the Useful Addresses section.

Packaging and brand identity

Fairly regularly, consumers' associations and environmental groups lambast retailers for selling products that are, in their opinion, grossly over-packaged. This is a little unfair – for two reasons. Firstly the packaging is, for the most part, provided by the manufacturers, not the retailers. Secondly the fact is that most consumers buy with their eyes. The product packaging that attracts their attention, and protects their purchase throughout its life, is therefore *extremely important*. Specialist agencies exist that will create or develop a brand's distinct personality, making the packaging an integral part of the product, rather than an afterthought.

Packaging and brand identity specialists work at harnessing customer interest through eye-catching and appropriate design; they try to create 'shelf impact' and an easily identifiable brand personality (for example, Mars bars, Marmite, Golden Syrup, or Perrier).

Sometimes their brief is to create a brand from scratch, to research the designated market and create a brand personality that will encourage potential customers to try it. More often they are asked to refresh an existing brand, to ensure that it remains up-to-date and that its existing and potential customer base does not tire of it (thus losing market share to competing products). At the same time they must ensure that the updated image is still recognisable to customers as the brand they know and love. For example, in recent years the packaging for Ovaltine, Marmite and Force Flakes have all been updated, without losing the essential brand image that customers can identify quickly in shops.

It is notoriously difficult for manufacturers – totally

immersed in the product and its history as they must be – to understand the key characteristics of a brand, and how that brand is perceived by the customer. An objective brand development agency can distil the essential qualities of a particular product's value to the market (perhaps its high-tech or gentle nature; its price advantage or style) and use this information to create a revitalised, fresh and up-to-date image. Brewer Riddiford (see Useful Addresses) is an agency that specialises in this area.

Brand naming agencies

Finding the right brand name is seldom as simple as it sounds. A good brand name should be memorable, strategically appropriate and legal; ideally forming the basis of a registered trademark. This is difficult, particularly in today's global market when advertisers often want the same advertising message to work worldwide (so it is vital to ensure that the term you adopt is not offensive and has no unpleasant connotations in any relevant language or culture). Kodak was one of the first companies to consider the strategic importance of the brand name. Theirs was invented by the company's founder, George Eastman, in 1888:

> I devised the name myself. The letter 'K' had been a favourite with me – it seems a strong, incisive sort of letter . . . It became a question of trying out a great number of combinations of letters that made words starting and ending with 'K'. The word 'Kodak' is the result. (Letter to Samuel Crowther of *System* magazine, 1920.)

His subsequent explanation of his thinking sounds very modern: 'There is, you know, a commercial value in having a peculiar name; it cannot be imitated or counterfeited.' (Letter to Mr G.W. Hunt of New York, 15 September 1888.)

Later, in 1906, he recalled that the name was:

> arrived at after considerable search for a word that would answer all requirements for a trademark name. The princi-

pal of these were that it must be short; incapable of being misspelled so as to destroy its identity; must have a vigorous and distinctive personality; and must meet the requirements of the various foreign trademark laws. (Letter to Mr John M. Manley, University of Chicago, 15 December 1906.)

Eastman was right – a name that is snappy and memorable, yet means nothing in any known language, has proved eminently suitable for building a worldwide brand.

Naming agencies can provide a brand identity for anything from a product or service to an entire company. The agency will start by considering all aspects of the subject, from the company's current image, its strengths, weaknesses, markets and competitors, to key features and benefits of the product. Only after a great deal of detailed research does the actual name-generating start, guided by what David Lowings of Dragon International brand name specialists (see Useful Addresses) calls 'focused creativity'.

A shortlist of prospective names is subjected to a full identical screening search to ensure originality, and worldwide checks with international associates and via computer databases ensure that the selected term(s) have the desired image in every important market. The eventual shortlist of recommendations will be presented to the client, fully supported by advice on design and product presentation. For example, ICI recently renamed their pharmaceutical division 'Zeneca', a made-up name selected from many, presumably because it sounds appropriately futuristic and high-tech.

Public relations

PR advice normally covers two areas: the promotion of a company's products (known as **consumer PR**); and/or the promotion of a corporate image (known as **corporate PR**).

In the early to mid-1980s there was an explosive growth of public relations specialists as professionals in their own right. Prior to this, PR activity was usually considered part of the role of the general advertising agency. The functions of advertising and editorial departments were more clearly distinguished in those days. Advertisers usually got their message across by taking advertising space (rather than trying to get editorial coverage), and newspaper proprietors seemed to be more conscious of the relationship between the advertising sales department (which effectively paid for the newspaper) and the editorial department, which reported the news.

Then the distinctions began to blur. As the price of advertising went up, advertisers began to demand more for their money. They wanted editorial coverage too, and no longer saw space advertising as their only – or even their best – option. At the same time, the newspapers were hungrier for stories and saw PR agencies as a cheap source of news and features. But with an increasingly competitive and unscrupulous press many firms felt they needed advice on how to secure positive media coverage. Hence the rush in the early 1980s to sign up with the increasing number of (sometimes self-styled) PR specialists.

By the late 1980s the situation had changed again. The effects of recession were making companies consider their budgets much more closely. Many firms, particularly smaller companies, started to question whether they were really receiving value for money from their public relations advisers. The key PR firm directors would visit for the pitch, but would never be seen again thereafter. The client would then have to spend time briefing a junior staff member on what made their kind of business tick, and in the meantime have to write their own press releases. What often annoyed them even more was having to send out the eventual release on the agency's (rather than their own) headed paper.

There are good reasons for insisting on routing every contact through the agency rather than the individual firm. It's usually easier to allow someone else to blow your trumpet than to do it yourself, and journalists who are used to dealing with personnel at a particular PR agency might find it confusing to find them listed at a manufacturer's address. But it is not hard to understand the resentment of smaller firms who felt they were effectively paying to promote their PR agency.

Today the PR industry has settled down and stratified a little. There are a number of large PR firms who deal with blue chip accounts (e.g. Shandwick, Lowe Bell and Burson-Marsteller). At the same time there has been a proliferation in the number of smaller specialist firms who deal with specific types of media. For example, there are agencies who specialise in helping clients promote financial services through the professional press and others who work within an organisation to handle media matters. And rather than appointing a PR firm on a rolling contract basis, year on year, it's possible to appoint them for a specific contract, renewable by mutual consent. The Public Relations Consultants Association Ltd (see Useful Addresses) offers an information service for potential clients of PR firms.

Sponsorship

A growing area of late has been the development of sponsorship opportunities, which many firms have seen as an ideal way to link a particular product with a specific market, particularly if the opportunities for straightforward advertising have been limited by central government. For example, tobacco and alcohol companies have long pursued an association between themselves and sport. More recently, specific products have been linked through sponsorship with television programmes – anything from light entertainment to news and weather. As a starting point for sponsorship enquiries, ask for the *Hollis Sponsorship Yearbook* in your local library. (See Further Reading.)

Along similar lines, in the film industry it has been possible for some time to pay for **product placement** (the inclusion of certain branded goods in films). The same opportunity is now being offered in some novels, where in return for a fee readers may hear about the specific brand of goods being used: e.g. 'she put on her Armani coat', or 'he gave her a huge diamond ring from Tiffany's'. Many of the agents of key sporting or media personalities will also negotiate endorsement deals, whereby a product is publicly used or praised in return for a fee.

Services related to direct marketing

Direct marketing is discussed in detail in Chapter 8. I'd just like to mention here that this area of marketing has spawned a huge variety of different service companies. You can, if you wish, instruct a single direct marketing agency to handle every aspect of a campaign, from list selection and copywriting to design and fulfilment. Alternatively you can instruct different specialists in each area (there are many individuals or smaller organisations working in the industry who are happy to liaise with each other on your behalf).

There is a wide variety of other services on offer too. For example, if you hold in-house mailing lists an analysis service can reveal exactly who you have on file, breaking down your potential customers into as many as 40 different socio-economic groupings. You can instruct a specialist tele-marketing agency to conduct a sales campaign for you, and a database management company to look after your list and its development. All these firms allow companies to experiment – and succeed – with direct marketing without taking on all the overheads for the various functions needed at the same time. These services continue because many firms eventually decide that it is more cost-effective to continue buying in expertise when they need it, rather than building it up from scratch themselves. A good starting point for exploring services available is to contact the Direct Marketing Association (see Useful Addresses) or to leaf through the advertisements in one of the trade journals such as *Direct Response*. Additionally, each Spring the Direct Marketing Fair at Olympia attracts exhibitors from all sectors of the industry.

Management consultants

The early 1980s saw the public emergence of a new type of marketing professional: the management consultant. It's a general term, and one that has often attracted sceptical press coverage.

Management consultants specialise in taking an objective look at a business, and how it is run, with a view to achieving measured improvement of performance in the future. They aim to provide 'business solutions'. They analyse the market sector involved and the company's position within it, set objectives and work out a structured plan to achieve them.

Consultants aim to recommend solutions that work in a variety of different ways: strategically, bearing in mind the company's desired future; operationally, according to the resources available; technically and culturally, within the organisation involved. The last point is particularly important. The management consultant should always match the ethos of the company; there is no point in recommending solutions on an ICI scale if the company is small and does not plan immediate and extensive investment.

It is equally important for the firm commissioning the work to have a clear idea of what they want from the consultant. What are you trying to achieve? What are the terms of reference? (Exactly what do you want them to look into and why?) If you make the brief too wide you could end up examining the symptoms rather than the cause. Just as important is the level at which the consultancy is commissioned. Does that person have the power to implement the results? If not, you are wasting money.

The great advantage of management consultants is the objective view they are able to provide. Lacking long experience of the individual company, they usually bring an experienced overview of the sector in general, and are thus well placed to advise on internal strengths and weaknesses, as well as external opportunities and threats.

A recent survey of management consultancies and their clients, carried out by Manchester Business School, revealed a subtle difference between the reasons companies hire consultants and the reasons consultants believe they are hired. A total of 87 per cent of the respondents cited special expertise and their need for an external point of view as the main reasons for seeking help from consultants. (Only 1.8 per cent said they were looking for 'new, original ideas'.) Consultancy firms, interviewed separately for the study, cited their experience in the client's business sector as their main strength in pursuing business.

A recurring theme throughout the study was the value of clear communication: 'what users want is not management jargon, but practically based expertise, clearly communicated'. This may be so, but it's an area that seems to sprout terminology. So, to bring you up to date, here is a short paragraph on the latest 'hot topic' involving management consultants – **business process re-engineering (BPR)**.

Consultants are often brought in to review the way internal company processes are carried out (e.g. how sales order processing leads towards order fulfilment). The aim is to simplify the process, shortening the time, and identifying the 'barriers' (such as the transfer of overall responsibility from one department to another) which can delay and add cost to the overall process. BPR fits in with the best aims of management consultancy – to provide an objective overview and make recommendations on how to improve operation.

Where do management consultants come from? There are large firms who can supply whole teams of people to work together for you (for example, Andersen Consulting have over 29,000 professionals operating from 157 offices in 45 countries). Many such firms have grown out of existing financial entrées into business, such as auditing and accounting services. In addition there are many individuals who work in specific areas of industry, largely recommended through word of mouth. The Institute of Management Consultants (see Useful Addresses) can provide a shortlist of qualified, professional consultants for specific projects.

Freelance help

There are certain areas of marketing expertise where, instead of relying on an agency to provide everything, you can coordinate the services of several self-employed individuals (freelances).

The most obvious examples are designers and copywriters, who can prepare the images and words for your promotional campaigns, but you may also find individuals to help with market research, statistical analysis and many other functions. The freelance network tends to work well and often in loose association; find a good copywriter and they usually have a favourite designer they like to work with. The benefits to you can be a very cost-effective service; individuals working at home have very low overheads. If you have no leads try the reference section of your local library for directories, or *Yellow Pages*. Alternatively, ask your job counterpart in other local companies (not direct competitors) whom they would recommend.

Designers

Help with design can come in many different forms, from a specialist department within an all-service agency to an individual offering freelance help as and when you need it. I have looked at the importance of design, and how to get the best out of the external help you employ, in Chapter 7.

And lots more . . .

In this chapter I have given just a taste of the wide variety of marketing services on offer. There are lots more, each area offering its own particular (and usually complex) vocabulary.

There are agencies who will organise your external functions – anything from the launch of a new product to a sales conference or exhibition. If your company is feeling a little long in the tooth and directionless, there are agencies who offer 'image assessment and identity development' to help you assess 'global trends' and decide which way to head in the future. If you are feeling even less well organised, there are firms who specialise in offering you 'crisis management' and training for the future. There are companies who can develop potential new products for you; and others who can make promotional videos to show to your reps or in retail outlets that stock your products. Still others will record the advertising (and other) output of your competitors or prepare your reports to shareholders.

If you can think of it, someone probably offers it. (A good starting point for finding out who offers what is the comprehensive advertising, laid out directory style, in *PR Week*, or contact the Public Relations Consultants Association – see Useful Addresses.) It's worth bearing in mind that all these service companies would much prefer you to see them as an investment in the future profitability of your business rather than just as a cost. The question you have to consider is how much marketing initiative you wish to consign to third parties.

How to be the perfect client

There are lots of books today on how best to manage your in-house staff. However the same rules apply when those you are dealing with are rewarded by a cheque from your accounts department rather than by a month's salary – don't assume that paying an invoice cancels out the human aspects of the job.

Most service companies accept that if anything goes well the client will put it down to the excellence of the product, and if the opposite happens it is likely to be recorded as the service company's fault. So a little bit of specific praise now and again can work a treat – and produce a much more motivated service in future. Remember that most marketing service companies that are any good eventually reach the happy state of being able to choose the accounts on which they work – difficult clients may risk being dropped.

Having commissioned help from a marketing service company, do listen to the advice you have paid for. It sometimes happens that the external consultant comes up with a solution other than the view that prevails in-house. If this does occur, it is not done out of sheer perversity. It is fairly common to hear of suppliers being paid a small percentage of their eventual fee for the initial mould-breaking research; far more of the budget is spent thereafter on hand-holding whilst selling the idea in-house. As George Riddiford, of Brewer Riddiford puts it:

The perfect client knows what he or she wants but not what it looks like. They may know they want to buy a suit to wear for an important occasion, but they need the specialist advice of the tailor or couturier to make it look just right.

In other words they accept that a solution to the problem exists, but cannot find it on their own. Such an approach brings the recognition and cooperation that is likely to produce the most effective results.

SUMMARY

There is a huge variety of different marketing services on offer. The basic requirements for those commissioning external advice and help may be summed up as follows:

- Be clear about what you want suppliers to do for you.
- Define the scope and limits of their activity.
- Establish how to implement agreed recommendations.

If you are unclear about any of these fundamental points you are probably wasting your money.

7

Doing the Work Yourself

PROVIDED YOU HAVE sufficient funds available, you can commission most of the elements of a marketing campaign from a variety of suppliers outside your organisation. In which case why bother to read this chapter? There are two main reasons.

Firstly, if you possess a basic understanding of how to do it yourself, you will save money. Apart from simply managing without external help from time to time (which will of course ease immediate strain on the budget), understanding how much work is involved in a project, what a supplier needs from you in order to do a good job, and providing the necessary support quickly will also save you money in the long run. Why?

To begin with, you will be able to estimate what a job should be costing you, and get good value for money. Also, suppliers get a nose for customers who waste their time and try to charge accordingly. Some agencies work out their quote and then add a percentage for the 'hassle factor' they expect. Others will pass on the extra time they spend through increased correction/administration charges. More expensive still, if their price was good and you prove a difficult customer: they may not want to work for you again.

Secondly, your understanding of the processes involved will help you get the results you want. Informed clients are more discerning. They are better able to instruct their suppliers and therefore stand a much greater chance of achieving their goals.

For guidance on planning your precise marketing obj

tives, see Chapters 3 and 4. And of course the principles described in the previous chapter apply whether you are commissioning the activities described or carrying them out yourself. In this chapter I'm going to concentrate on the two main elements of the promotion piece – copy (the words you use to convey your sales message) and design.

COPY

What is good copy?

Promotional copy is written with one purpose in mind: to persuade the customer to buy. It may try to do this by entertaining you, shocking you, persuading you or shouting at you, but if you do not respond by feeling any interest in the product, and you are part of the designated market, then the advertisement has failed, and the copy is poor.

Once you appreciate this basic rule, some advertisements can make you feel hugely superior. You may have enjoyed a television commercial for an estate car, and understood that its budget was probably greater than that for the entire programme that surrounded it, yet if you can't remember what brand it was advertising a couple of hours later, and you are potentially in the market for such a vehicle, then it has failed. You will soon appreciate that vast amounts of money get misspent or just wasted in this area.

Just as the marketing led company is more concerned with the market and their needs than their own manufacturing capabilities, so *good copy concentrates on the customer* rather than the company doing the selling. It talks about market needs, not company organisation. It doesn't use jargon or terms which the market may not understand, and it provides all the information they need to take the next step.

The recent press and poster advertising campaign by the Advertising Standards Authority makes an interesting example of this. The initial assumption that the ads are displaying information that the organisation – rather than the customer – finds interesting, is not as simple as it at first seems.

The ads all featured a series of series of rather menacing-looking faces and the following words:

ASA☑
KEEPING
TABS
ON ADS

The text was difficult to read because the words were in capital letters, which are hard to read in a hurry (and don't we all read most ads in a hurry?). Also, it was not immediately apparent what was being promoted – my first reaction was that it was an advert for the supermarket ASDA who have a store in my neighbourhood. But even if you did know that ASA stood for Advertising Standards Authority, and that they were the people to contact if you felt an advertisement was incorrect or misleading, the one thing you would most likely want to know is where to find them. At the time, the ad contained no address or telephone number; not even an instruction you might remember such as 'look in the phone book', and it was this apparent lack of market orientation that attracted some criticism in the press.

Interestingly the ASA, when offered the chance to comment on the advertisements, revealed a rather different marketing objective. The ads were designed to raise the organisation's profile, rather than encourage more complaints. Consistent surveys have revealed a very high awareness of the ASA's function; they get a great many members of the public contacting them to complain. Although their telephone lines are always busy, they can in fact investigate only *written* complaints. (This is why more recent versions of the ad have included only the address of the organisation, not its telephone number.)

The ASA planned that frequent appearance of the advertisements would boost recognition of both the image and the organisation behind it. It is also worth noting that the ASA do not pay for any of the space taken to display the ads. All sectors of the advertising industry take part in drawing up and implementing the self-regulatory code, and free display, usually as 'filler' ads when space occurs, is part of the industry's commitment to that code.

Another fundamental point that needs to be made immediately is that we are talking about *copy, not writing*, as learnt at school. Promotional copy seeks to get a message across, and in achieving this goal all techniques are legitimate. You can start sentences with 'and' or 'but', and you can miss out the verb altogether if the sentence makes sense without it. These are all techniques at your disposal to serve the wider aim of attracting attention to the product you are promoting. Forget the précis skills you acquired in English lessons and repeat your basic sales message as often as you need to, each time using slightly different words. Bearing in mind where your copy is to appear, it should be as long as it needs to be to convince the market and motivate a purchase. A common mistake is to write too little.

The only basic grammatical rule you should observe in promotional copy is not to use a split infinitive. It is, in fact, perfectly correct grammar, but for some reason using one is like waving a red flag at a bull. People will stop attending to your message and congratulate themselves on catching you out.

For the same reasons, forget the lofty style that impressed your teachers at school and get on with what the market wants to know about the product. As Aldous Huxley observed, back in 1927:

> . . . any trace of literariness in an advertisement is fatal to its success. Advertisement writers may not be lyrical, or obscure, or in any way esoteric. They must be universally intelligible. A good advertisement has this in common with drama and oratory, that it must be immediately comprehensible and directly moving.

So, how do you write good selling copy? Firstly by grasping

an essential principle: good copy is easy to read; it is seldom easy to write.

Where to start

Don't start by writing

Instead, think about the project in its widest sense. What are you trying to achieve? It is so easy to plump for a familiar promotional format and start scribbling without pausing to think things through. Do you really need the leaflet you are about to write? Will producing a full-colour brochure for a product being promoted as good value make the market conclude that it is over-priced? Do you need a letter *and* a leaflet?

Start with total market immersion (TMI)

Understand how the product works and what it offers, but then spend even more time thinking about the market for the product rather than the product itself. Concentrate on the customer's need, not on your need to tell. You may find that your product meets market needs even though no one has thought to tell the market before. For example, there are certain breakfast cereals that have always been high in fibre, even before it became a key selling point.

Stand back from the project and ask yourself the questions that any good copywriter would insist were part of the brief:

- What is it?
- What does it do?
- What does it replace/improve on?
- Who will buy/use it?
- What sort of job do they have? What kind of person are they?

- What does this kind of person currently use instead?
- What alternatives do they have?
- How do they like to buy (through the post, in supermarkets or specialist shops)?

Consider, too, how much the market already knows. Are you trying to inform a market that already knows and likes your product or are you talking to people who have never come across it before? The tone adopted and the type of information included for these two groups need to be very different.

Absorb as much marketing information as possible

Don't confine your study of possible promotional formats to your competitors' leaflets. There are two main reasons for this.

Firstly, advertising works best if it is slightly surprising: we don't read what we think we already know. It stands to reason, therefore, that you have a better chance of attracting attention if your promotional material doesn't look exactly like that of your competitors. So don't just look at home for inspiration. Subscribe to the general marketing press, not just the trade press for your own industry. You'll find details of how other products get marketed fascinating – and it's always interesting to read about the campaigns that *don't* work!

Secondly, the people who buy your product don't only buy from your own industrial sector; they are exposed to, and respond to, a vast range of other stimuli. People who buy highly technical equipment or have extremely demanding jobs also choose particular brands of aftershave and go to certain chain stores for their underwear. Or, as copywriter Roger Millington says, 'Everyone puts on their socks one foot at a time.'

So it makes sense to look at how other organisations attract our attention. How do supermarkets and garages persuade us to buy? Spot the relative readability of road signs on motorways (usually excellent) compared with posters that you see on billboards (hugely variable in their effectiveness). Get on as many mailing lists as possible and be critical about what you receive. Most professional copywriters have a 'swipe file' for examples they like. Watch out for formats that get used repeatedly, particularly if they carry a coupon – a sure sign that they are producing results.

Bear in mind how promotional copy gets read

Always remember that the only person who reads advertising copy through from start to finish is the person who wrote it; sometimes not even then, as anyone who has tried to proof-read their own work will agree (it's very easy to miss mistakes).

In reality our reading habits are extremely promiscuous. Think about how you look through a newspaper trawling for something to catch your eye. And yet, *having paid for it*, a newspaper is something that we are very motivated to read. Think how much harder advertising copy has to work to get read.

When faced with a new advertisement, if they bother to read it at all, most people do the following:

- First they look at the headline.

- Then they look at the bottom of the page to see who is advertising.

- If there is a photograph, they read the caption.

- Only after this will they look at the general text, most usually by looking at the paragraph headings first rather than reading the text itself.

This means that the information presented in these places is absolutely vital. A strong headline can grasp the reader's attention and get them reading the rest of the advertisement; while an effective 'signing-off block' at the bottom can restate the main product benefits and urge the reader to buy the product. Captions provide a quick way of finding out what the copy is all about and so, at the very least, should contain the product's chief selling points. Break up explanatory copy (usually called 'body copy') into enticingly small amounts, make it interesting to read, and you are more likely to motivate a purchase.

It sounds obvious but I will say it anyway: the headline should go at the top of the page or space. Flick through any recent newspaper or magazine and you will see how your eye is attracted to the bold headline, *wherever it appears*. If it is placed in the middle of the page, and is sufficiently interesting for you to carry on reading the rest of the text, you will find yourself reading what is immediately beneath the heading, having missed half the explanatory copy. Why pay for wasted space?

Never look at a proof of an ad you are placing on its own; have a copy of the magazine or journal next to you and see what else is likely to appear near it. Your high-priced space will not lie in isolation on your customers' desks asking to be read!

As they look at the open pages of a newspaper or magazine, most people's eyes sweep across from left to right (this seems to apply to both left- and right-handed people). It follows that it's easier to get noticed on the right-hand side of the page than the left, so when booking advertising space always ask for a right-hand page, preferably facing editorial rather than other advertising material (don't *you* skip past double pages of advertising?). Pay attention to any particular spots in the publication you want to appear in that are particularly noted by readers (e.g. next to the crossword, above the births, marriages and deaths column, and so on).

Write from memory

Make notes as you do your research, and make a list of headings or areas that your final material should cover, but when it comes to the actual composition, you should always write from memory.

With some 40,000 square miles of Great Lakes waters to enjoy it's hardly surprising that water-based sports such as swimming, sailing and windsurfing are so popular.

Michigan's boathouses and harbours shelter more than 22,000 boats, and on a drive along one of the well-marked scenic routes encircling the lakes it's never long before another handful of masts appears between the trees.

On a drive through Michigan the chances are you'll pass more boats than you will cars.

MEMBER OF THE GREAT LAKES OF N. AMERICA

Of course Michigan isn't only about water, there are the beautiful old towns, world class golf courses and our glorious national forests to explore too.

For a free information pack send the coupon to Michigan Information Centre, 110 St. Martin's Lane, LONDON WC2N 4DY, or call 0171 240 1422.

> NAME: _____
>
> ADDRESS: _____
>
> _____
>
> _____ POSTCODE: _____
>
> # MICHIGAN
>
> HEART OF THE GREAT LAKES

There are dangers in placing the headline for an advertisement anywhere other than at the top of the copy – you risk distracting the reader away from a substantial part of your sales message. But just to show that there are no absolute rules in advertising, the smaller illustration above the headline does serve to direct the eye back up towards the beginning of the copy again.

The Do's and Don'ts of The Lands' End Experience.

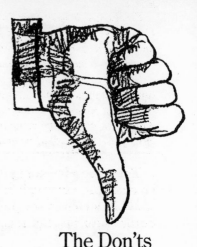

The Do's

1. Call us free on 0800 220 106, seven days a week, 24 hours a day (except Christmas Day).

2. Ask for our free catalog featuring many hundreds of items of classic clothing for men, women and kids.

3. Order something and, in most cases, if we have it in stock, we ship it to you in just a few short days.

4. Whatever it is, you can be sure it's of top quality, and it comes with our one word guarantee. GUARANTEED.

5. You enjoy true value because we're Direct Merchants. No middlemen take their cuts on the route from us to you.

6. You begin receiving our catalogs regularly once we receive your request.

Best of all, once you've given us your name and your order, you've opened the door to the downright, down-to-earth pleasure of the Lands' End Experience. We're more than a catalog and a warehouse. We're friends not just out to make a sale to you, but to build a lasting relationship.

Why not give us a try?

The Don'ts

1. You don't leave the comfort of your home.

2. You don't fight your way through crowded car parks.

3. You don't elbow your way through impatient shopping crowds.

4. You don't wait for a bored assistant to commune with his or her computer.

5. You don't get clamped.

6. You don't pay parking.

7. You don't burn petrol.

8. You don't lose patience.

©1995 Lands' End Inc.

Don't miss another Lands' End catalog.

Do send for your FREE catalog now, by calling us on FREEPHONE 0800 220 106, *quoting reference XG.* Or mail this coupon or FREE FAX us on 0800 222 106.

Name _____
(Mr/Mrs/Miss/Ms.)
Address _____

_____ Postcode _____ XG

Send to: Lands' End Direct Merchants UK Limited, FREEPOST, Pillings Road, Oakham, Rutland LE15 6NY.
From time to time we make portions of our mailing list available to carefully selected organizations whose products may be of interest to you. If you would prefer not to receive such mailings, please tick this box. ☐

OPPOSITE: This advertisment produced by a firm selling high quality casual clothing direct to customers illustrates a number of interesting points.

Firstly, just look at how far the medium of catalogue selling has come. Once largely the preserve of firms selling goods through commission on an instalment basis to lower socio-economic groups, now it has fully emerged as a sophisticated and convenient way of buying.

Secondly, note how the copy neatly turns each feature of the company's organisation into a customer benefit and creates a strong and reassuring feeling of belonging to a club. The copy confirms your good judgement about the company and its products; the basis on which buying decisions would be made.

The reason for doing this is that your copy is more likely to be personal; you explain as you go along. Good copy should read like a chat in the pub, not an exchange of literary letters destined for posthumous publication!

How to write effective copy

Copywriters love to condense their aims into acronyms. Many of these may be familiar to you already but they are worth restating.

AID(C)A

Invented over 50 years ago, **AIDA** is one of the best-known advertising acronyms. Originally developed as a formula for writing direct mail shots, it works equally well for press advertisements, leaflets, telemarketing scripts and other promotional formats. It was recently updated, with the addition of a **C**, and now stands for: **Attract, Interest, Desire, Conviction, Action**.

These are the five stages you should take your market through. **Attract** gains attention; **interest** keeps it going; **desire** kindles the need to own. **Conviction** is the proof – perhaps a third party opinion or a guarantee. **Action** asks for the order.

ONE MILLION OF YOU ARE LOOKING AT THIS.

Dancer Rehearsing Juliet.
Original screenprint by
Donald Hamilton Fraser R.A. £195.

ONLY 295 OF YOU CAN OWN IT.

Every CCA Galleries print is part of a strictly limited edition, personally numbered and signed by the artist – in this case, Donald Hamilton Fraser R.A. whose work has been shown extensively both here and in the USA.

This exclusivity, thankfully, is not reflected in the cost – prices start from around a modest £50.

——— ◇ ———

To reserve your free colour copy of the Portfolio,
just return the coupon below. Today.
Or 'phone us on 01-491 2523 (24 hours).

——— ◇ ———

Exhibitions of Donald Hamilton Fraser's prints and paintings open at all our Galleries commencing 1st November 1989.
For more information call 01-499 6701.

——— ◇ ———

To: CCA Galleries Ltd , Freepost, 8 Dover Street, London W1X 3PJ.

NAME _____

ADDRESS _____

POSTCODE _____

CCA GALLERIES
LONDON OXFORD BATH FARNHAM

ID2/10/89

This CCA Gallery advertisement is an excellent illustration of the principles of **AIDCA**. The headline **attracts interest** and kindles the **desire** to own, which is further developed in the body copy. The strategy is based on a very simply piece of market research: finding out what the paper's readership on that day was likely to be, and offering something that would not be available to everyone who wanted it. **Conviction** or proof of the desirability of what is on offer is confirmed by the information that the artist has exhibited extensively in both the UK and the USA. The call to **action** is the 24-hour telephone number and the coupon. This is a very effective use of space.

Think back to the Advertising Standards Authority poster (see page 123). It attracted attention and was perhaps interesting but took the reader no further.

FAB

FAB stands for **Features**, **Advantages** and **Benefits**. This is a useful checklist to ensure that your copy is relevant and interesting to the market. Many copywriters get no further than listing features. These need to be converted into what really interests the reader: benefits. Here's an example:

New Pookins Washing Powder contains newly researched ingredient XPZ2. (**Feature**)

Which reaches deep down into the dirt trapped in the fibres of your clothes. (**Advantage**)

Which means you get a whiter wash without having to run everything through the machine twice. (**Benefit**)

To check that you are describing benefits not features, ask yourself 'which means what?' after each sales point. If the answer is not clear you still need to explain the benefit.

You may argue that intelligent consumers can work out the benefits for themselves. But why should they bother? If you are trying to sell your product you need to be sure that your sales message is completely understood. The principle of selling benefits not features is summed up in the advertising maxim: 'sell the sizzle, not the sausage'.

USP

A **USP** (**Unique Selling Proposition**) is what makes a product different from everything else on the market. The demand for USPs was at its height in the advertising industry in America in the 1950s – if one was not immediately apparent it had to be invented.

Here are some examples of the USP providing an identity for products that are in reality very similar to others on the market:

Tesco: Every little helps.

British Airways: The world's favourite airline.

Milky Way: The chocolate you can eat between meals without ruining your appetite.

Today the USP is no longer so widespread. Some items (known as 'me too' products) are deliberately very similar to their competitors and are best promoted on the basis of similarity and value for money. But if what you are promoting is unique (new to the market, a completely new look at the subject, new format, etc), make sure you tell the market.

WIIFM

WIIFM means **What's in it for me?** Any piece of copy, on any subject whatever, should always make this clear to the designated market. *Don't* be ambiguous or clever.

Another test of whether or not the message is coming across clearly is to say 'so what?' at the end of every paragraph of copy. If the answer is unclear, then strike it out.

KISS

One last acronym. Remember that in order to provide swift access to information, your text should be as clear as possible. Or, as someone else summed it up, **KISS – Keep it simple, stupid**.

Use attention-grabbing headlines

Advertisements attract attention if the copy is, or looks, personal and relevant. So if you are writing for a specific market, name it:

Calling all teenagers!

Important information for all English teachers.

Then target the benefits to your audience as specifically as possible.

One of the most reliable techniques for starting a head-line is to ask a question: Why? What? Where? How? Who? When? This can give you headlines that get straight to the point:

How this course will save you time and money.

Why everyone is talking about this new video.

You could start your headline by saying something controversial, preferably to stimulate debate rather than cause outright denial and make the reader look away. The highly controversial Benetton poster advertisements of 1993–4 are an interesting illustration of this point (although, admittedly, they were almost entirely copy-free). Designed to make the company look socially aware and to appeal to the younger generation, images such as a newborn baby, the bloodied clothes of a dead Yugoslav soldier or an AIDS victim on the point of death, got a great amount of attention but caused outcry and widespread revulsion. In Germany, Benetton's central management were charged by a group of individual franchise holders with bringing the company's image into disrepute, resulting in sharply reduced profits in stores.

You should also try to use catchwords that are instantly interesting. Words like:

Now	Unique
Free	Money off
Introducing	Save Sale
Announcing	Offer closes
Secret	Guarantee
Magic	Bargain
Mother	

It's often a good idea to include a promise:

A completely new kind of health manual: satisfaction or your money back.

Using an informative, news-presenting tone, or featuring a new way of using the product can also be effective:

Why each year over 1,000 people needlessly die.

If you are mailing your information, put an attention-grabbing headline on the envelope. State your best offer or start a story but leave it unfinished so the reader is encouraged to open up and carry on reading:

How spending £500 on our new training package will help your company save thousands more . . .

Blind headlines (which can only be understood once the rest of the copy has been read) are best avoided. If the meaning isn't clear most readers won't bother to read on. For a similar reason, you should delete introductory sentences which say more about the writer's need to feel at home with the subject than the reader's need to know. For example, if writing to extremely clever research biochemists:

'Microbiochemistry is one of the fastest expanding areas of scientific research today.'

(WIIFM? So what?)

Finally, avoid humour in copywriting unless you are very sure it works.

Get to the point

Think how you respond to a telesalesperson who won't get to the point about what the 'special promotion on offer in your area for a very limited time only . . .' is. We are all busy and haven't got the time (or inclination) to work out for ourselves why the call is being made. Think how supermarkets save us time by identifying the location of every kind of product under one of about 30 in-store headings.

Make your text easy to read

Check for readability by reading it aloud (seriously). Better still, get someone else to read it aloud to you – this will show up any words or phrases that are difficult. (These are most likely to be the phrases you are particularly proud of; the bits your fond eye keeps roving back to as really good examples of your writing style!)

The urge to alter someone else's copy must be one of the hardest temptations to resist. Faced with almost any piece of text, one can always think of a better way of wording it. When others try to change what you have written, do try to distinguish between valid criticism of your hard-wrought prose and the desire to meddle. Being objective about your own work will help you when you come to commissioning copy from freelances.

Keep to short words, not long ones ('news' not 'information'; 'now' not 'currently'; 'show' not 'demonstrate'). The first sentence should be short (the advertising guru, David Ogilvy, reckons no more than 11 words) but after that you should vary the length of your sentences and paragraphs, avoiding the very long and indigestible. One-word sentences work well. Really. But just to prove that there are exceptions to any rule, the occasional long or difficult word can be very effective if carefully chosen (for example, the recent television advertisements for Phileas Fogg snacks and After Eight chocolate mints illustrate the humorous use of long words).

Along the same lines, try to use vivid terms, not hackneyed ones: 'hate' instead of 'dislike'; 'adore' instead of 'love'. Write in the present tense, using active not passive verbs ('you can buy', not 'this can be bought'). Better still, use an imperative ('Buy!').

Linking phrases help your copy flow, for example:

You can see that . . .	After all . . .
And of course . . .	Just as important . . .
At the same time . . .	For example . . .
Not to mention . . .	This includes . . .
Did you realise . . .	In addition . . .
So that . . .	On the other hand . . .
In order to . . .	Finally I must mention . . .
As you can see . . .	A final point . . .

Make your text chatty and personal. Try to imagine one of your target customers and write specifically to them – your copy will sound more personal then. (This is why most of the round-robin Christmas letters enclosed with cards are so boring – they are very impersonal.) Overcome any objections the customer may think of as you write, incorporating them naturally within your sales text.

Don't be clever or pompous, even when you are writing to an audience that is either or both. Imagine you are explaining the benefits to a prospect face to face; you would be concentrating on the product, not your presentational style. Give facts not opinions, unless they are the opinions of a third party who is respected by the market.

Write in the present tense and get the word 'you' in as often as possible – it changes the way you write. For example, which of the following sentences has more impact?

The eggs found in dog faeces can cause blindness in children.

Your child could be blinded by the eggs found in dog faeces.

Asking a question, particularly a controversial or newsworthy one, is a good way to attract attention:

Do you realise that the eggs found in dog faeces can cause blindness in children?

Don't bore the reader

Avoid the predictable. Clichés make the reader switch off, as do overused words such as 'wonderful', 'timely', 'amazing'.

Constantly repeating your company name or product title is another common mistake. You may think you are reinforcing the words in the market's mind. In fact exactly the opposite happens. Usually the words are highlighted or underlined and the reader gets used to recognising a block of copy he or she has seen before and skipping past it. It may never get read.

The same goes for politicians who talk in threes:

> The policies that we agreed on; the policies that the nation approved in the ballot box; the policies that are right for Britain.

We can anticipate what is coming so we stop listening.

Equally boring to the market is irrelevant information about your company. The following is from a questionnaire I received from British Gas shortly after privatisation. The copy was centred on 'you', but conveyed information that they, rather than the reader, would have found interesting:

> Dear Customer
> You will probably have noticed the advertising about British Gas recently. We have talked about our determination to grow and develop our business, to protect the environment, to support the vital engineering and manufacturing base of our country, and to foster the communities we serve and on whom we depend.
>
> As a customer you were perhaps most interested in the 'Banishing Gripes' advertisement. In my new job as Chairman of British Gas, I want you to know that providing a high quality of service to our customer remains our top priority . . .

And so on . . .

Don't drone on about your company. The average reader

could not care less; it is the specific product that has attracted his or her attention. If there is information that is relevant to the product give it, but spare the reader the potted company history.

Don't oversell

When doing your research on the product it is useful to make a list of the selling points. But when it comes to drafting the copy you may not need to use them all. Having established all the sales benefits of the product you are promoting, rank them and use them in order: one idea per sentence; one theme per paragraph.

Qualify every statement and be specific

If you are imprecise, doubt may creep into the reader's mind as to the validity of your arguments. So, for example, instead of saying 'widely used in major companies', say 'in extensive use at IBM and BP'.

Avoid using negatives

Negatives weaken your message. For example, 'our product is good value' has a lot more impact than 'our product is not expensive'. They can also make your copy very confusing (unless of course that is your aim). How about this from the back of a leaflet distributed to expectant mothers by a firm that manufactures baby milk formula? I can't imagine any wording *less* likely to provide swift access to meaning!

> . . . Introducing partial bottle feeding could negatively affect breast feeding and reversing a decision not to breastfeed is difficult.

Be careful about knocking the opposition

This is probably the question I get asked most often – should you name the opposition? In some markets (such as Japan) knocking a competitor's product is illegal.

If your product has a material benefit not offered by the opposition, then it may well be in your interests to make the comparison. But do be careful. Make your point clearly (don't end up providing the competition with a free ad); make sure you are not being libellous; and be aware of the danger of destroying the market's confidence in any brand of the product in question, including your own. For example, the most likely result of the protracted controversy between Persil (Lever Brothers) and Ariel (Proctor & Gamble) over whether or not Persil Power rots clothes is a loss of consumer confidence in this market sector altogether.

Hang on to your first reaction

Incomprehensible copy received from another department will strike you as such the first time you read it. Hang on to that reaction and adapt the copy for the market outside your own company as soon as possible.

The more you read impenetrable copy, the more familiar you become with the words, the more you will start to assume that you know what it means. If you are told that the market understands highly technical language, be sure that this is really true. What about retailers, reps, journalists, librarians, secretaries, those standing in for others who are away on courses or leave of absence? Do they *all* understand too? For the same reason, don't use jargon. You may get it wrong, be misunderstood by your audience, or simply sound extremely patronising.

Make the customer an offer

More and more advertising material makes an offer to the audience, whether actual (free plastic model inside this cereal packet) or general ('we won't make a drama out of a crisis' – from an insurance company). Why don't you make one too?

Don't assume that offers are beneath your audience. Everyone today is motivated by the idea of getting something for nothing, and this includes the very clever and the very busy (who on average get fewer offers made to them). Offers can boost response, make the customer come back again sooner, and motivate a larger order. Look at the cosmetics companies offering a pack of goodies with two purchases; or the firms selling new kitchens that offer an additional discount if orders are received by a certain date. Offers get made because they work (ask anyone from Hoover).

Free gifts should be relevant to the market, not to the product you are selling. If you just want to dip your toe in the water, try experimenting with free postage and packing, or a percentage discount for responses received by a certain date, and see what happens.

Give a guarantee

Before committing yourself to anything, I bet *you* read the small print. So will your customers. *Response is always in inverse proportion to the amount of commitment asked for.* If you offer a cast iron guarantee your customers will feel more secure about ordering from you, and hence more willing to do so. Don't worry if one or two people take you up on the guarantee, as the increased level of orders should compensate. Handle the complainers sympathetically and you will probably have some even more loyal customers on your hands.

Use someone else's words rather than your own

This applies to all promotional literature *except* press releases where the use of quotation marks may give the impression that the story has already been covered. The 'someone' does not have to be famous, just someone credible. For example, it would be far more effective to have a head teacher or subject adviser endorsing an educational textbook rather than a famous footballer. And don't assume you have to pay for the words. If the person you approach genuinely likes your product, is sympathetic to your aims, and doesn't mind the publicity, they may well provide you with an endorsement for nothing. The writer and comedian, Stephen Fry, constantly plugs the Apple Macintosh (for nothing) because he believes it is a wonderful machine.

Similarly, review or feature quotations from the press are more valuable to the reader than your opinion, but when deciding which ones to use, choose those from the journals that are best-known to the market, even if they are slightly less complimentary than those that appeared in lesser-known titles. For similar reasons, choose national rather than local publications, unless you are selling to a local market.

Quotation marks at the top of an ad really attract attention. In *Ogilvy on Advertising*, David Ogilvy said they increase recall by 25 per cent. If you don't have a quotation to use, supply one yourself and put it in inverted commas to attract attention: 'How your company can benefit from the latest techniques in marketing'.

However, do take care that an endorsement doesn't actually deter people from buying. Pay attention to religious, political, sexual and other sensitivities. For similar reasons, pop stars have to pay attention to the public image of their private lives as they risk losing valuable endorsement contracts. (Allegations of child abuse against Michael Jackson may have affected his working relationship with Pepsi Cola.)

DESIGN

Good design for promotional purposes should be implicit, not explicit. If the customer starts admiring the layout, they have stopped thinking about the product, and that is dangerous.

Even if you manage without external help in most areas of your marketing, when it comes to design you will most probably need assistance of some sort. This may come from an in-house design department, a freelance designer, an external studio or just a friend of the printer's who, you have been told, has a 'good eye' for design. Here you come across people with a professional training you do not have. There are two very important factors to bear in mind.

Firstly, we are not talking about fine art, so you can forget 'artistic integrity', 'total vision' and all that jazz. What is important in promotional design is *getting a sales message across*. Some designers seem to hate words – a particularly difficult situation if they are working on promotional material.

Secondly, let's put design in its place. *Consideration of the market is critical*; far more important than the layout. Assuming the copy is right, the worst-designed promotional campaign in the world will still produce results if it is sent to the right market. The same is not true of the best-designed piece sent to the wrong market.

So, at the risk of all my designer friends never speaking to me again, your experience as a person who reads advertising material, and keeps your eyes open as you walk down the street, is extremely valid when deciding how effective particular designs are. Your role is that of the boy who pointed out that the Emperor's new clothes weren't there; in other words you can offer basic common sense.

Design is *not* simply a matter of taste; there are some very basic rules that need to be followed and which designers should break only in exceptional circumstances. Input from you will help cure any possible artistic excesses and produce something that is easy to read, remember and respond to.

What are the rules of good promotional design?

1   Make the copy easy to read

Copy set at an angle may be visually dynamic but is extremely hard to read. If the customer has to turn their page around to read your ad, will they bother?

Avoid fitting text around pictures. Returning to a different place on every line is tiring on the eye. The same goes for very wide text settings and text printed in clever shapes (telephones or maps of France in recent years). The eye gets tired, and tired eyes stop reading. Think about how you are able to scan down the middle of newspaper columns to grasp the essentials without reading the whole article. When your message is designed to sell it's even more important to make the text easy to read.

Lower-case letters are much easier to read than capitals – we are able to read them as groups, rather than spelling them out letter by letter. Why else would schools teach children to read in this way or the Department of Transport have all road signs (apart from the initial capitals) produced in lower case? It follows that if you put too much text in capitals, it will not get read.

Serif typefaces are easier to read than non-serif ones; the little tails help us grasp whole words more quickly.

Don't use too many typefaces or special effects – the effect can be very jarring. We've all seen a promotional piece produced in-house by someone who has just gained access to the desktop publishing system for the first time. The result can look more like a sampler to show what the machine is capable of than easy-to-read copy.

Reversing text out of a solid colour can be a good way to attract attention but is very hard on the eyes, so it's a technique that should only be used sparingly. Never reverse text out of a photograph – it's almost impossible to read.

2   Draw the eye in

It's the spaces in any piece of copy that draw the eye in. Don't justify your text (keep a ragged right-hand margin) and create interesting spaces by using:

- bullet points (beware of over-bulleting though)

sub-headings

> putting copy in a box, and if your material is to be
> printed putting a tint behind the box

  indenting text

numbering your paragraphs

occasional <u>underlining</u>

putting text in CAPITALS or *italics* (sparingly)

using tables and bar charts to divide up the copy

making the text 'run over' the end of a page so the reader is
encouraged to continue

3 Bear in mind where the advertisement is to be seen

If the market has little time to spare (e.g. the ad is appearing
on the backs of buses) it needs to be comprehensible at a
glance. If the market has more time available (e.g. when travelling on the underground) then longer copy can work very
well. Even on today's clogged roads I doubt that the car
driver has more than five seconds at his or her disposal to
read a poster. It is easier to get a message across if you use
strong, pure colours, rather than a 'muddy palette'.

4 Take great care with coupons and order forms

When it comes to coupons, ensure that these are large
enough – there's nothing more annoying than one that's too
small to fill in. Suggest that the designer lays out the coupon
first. Examples of excellent design to copy here are insurance
proposal forms, and the newly designed annual tax return.
Both give reversed-out white space for anything the
customer has to complete; you can see at a glance whether
all the required information has been given.

The order form should be on an edge, preferably the bottom right-hand edge of a right-hand page so that it can be cut out with the minimum of disruption to the text. Does it back on to another advertisement or on to text? If it backs on to another coupon, ask for your money back. With journals that are kept for reference, most readers will be unwilling to carve up portions of the text. Make sure you state that the order form can be photocopied or the item ordered by telephone or fax.

Ensure that your address and number for telephone orders appears on both the advertisement and the coupon. It sometimes happens that you cut out an order form to send, and then find the address is back on the main advertisement, in the magazine, wherever that is.

Make sure the telephone number is in very large print – that's the easiest way to order so make sure your customers realise they have that option. Likewise, freephone attracts attention and hence orders. Many companies now accept a huge percentage of their orders by fax, even from consumers at home.

How to find a designer

I've filled in forms over the years to get myself listed in directories of freelances, but I still find that the majority of my work comes through personal recommendation. And that's the method I've always found best for finding designers.

Good designers are not ten a penny. So if you do find a designer you enjoy working with, stick with them. Find someone who gets to know your work and will make constructive suggestions. A relationship like this has saved my bacon several times.

Lastly, I would apply the same rule to employing designers as any other freelance service – don't use too many suppliers. If you use a great many designers it's not only confusing trying to remember where each job is, you also prevent yourself being financially significant to any one of them – and hence denying them a major incentive to please you.

SUMMARY

The very best advertising copy and design is entirely unnoticed by the customer – he or she is too busy drooling over the product.

Good advertising should be easy to read and understand. Bearing in mind the place where the sales message is to appear, it should be as long as necessary to make all the relevant sales points, guiding the reader towards the next stage in the chain towards (repeat) purchase. Clear design gives the reader instant access to the message, helping him or her to assimilate and remember the sales points made.

8

Direct Marketing

WHEN, AT THE END of the 1970s, consumers first became aware that many businesses were using computers rather than individuals to manage their day-to-day dealings, there were lots of jokes doing the rounds about computer-generated mistakes. The most popular one was about someone who kept receiving a final demand for £0.00. He was told that it was a computer error, but when pursuit continued he eventually wrote a cheque for £0.00, only to be told by his bank that this had now messed up *their* computer. Such stories now seem archaic; today the computer is our servant, not our master.

I'm sure that in a few years many of the fables that surround direct marketing will sound similarly outdated. We've all head these opinions forcefully expressed: 'I hate junk mail'; 'No one reads it'; 'I open my post over a waste-paper basket'; and so on.

But just look how far the medium has come. Twenty years ago shopping by mail was mainly the preserve of catalogues offering those with low disposable income the chance to buy on the 'never never'. Today it's an extremely sophisticated method of marketing. More and more companies are exploring the option of selling direct, in an ever-increasing variety of ways: off-the-page advertising; telemarketing; party plan, and so on. What is more, we are all receiving more of it. In 1986–7 direct mail constituted 13 per cent of all letter mail. By 1991 the comparative figure had risen to 16 per cent. In 1985 the average person was receiving 4.1 items at home every four weeks; by 1994 this had risen to 6.3 items. Already, dinnerparty chatter tends to centre on the pervasive nature of the information retained by the marketers, rather than complaints about the receipt of direct marketing material in general.

	Volume of direct mail (million items)		
	Consumer	**Business**	**Total**
1988	1221	545	1766
1989	1445	672	2117
1990	1544	728	2272
1991	1435	687	2122
1992	1658	588	2246
1993	1772	664	2436
1994	2015	715	2730

Source: Royal Mail

The average household receives 6.3 items of direct mail every four weeks.

The average manager receives 15 items per week at work.

What exactly is direct marketing?

Direct marketing means selling direct to the end user or consumer, without the intervention of a middle man such as a retailer.

Direct marketing can be further subdivided into two kinds of activity. **Direct response** advertising seeks to promote, as the name implies, a response directly back to the promoter. For example, an advertisement in a Sunday supplement that asks you to ring a particular telephone number, and quote a specific reference number when ordering, is gauging the exact response to that advertisement in that issue of the newspaper.

Direct promotion advertisements may also invite a direct order, but their primary function is to spread information; the response may come back through a variety of other means or outlets. For example, a food manufacturer offering a money-off coupon through a women's magazine, which may be redeemed through any shop or supermarket stocking the goods, is an example of direct promotion. The recent printing of messages on eggs, targeted at the 'fridge-visiting audience', is another.

How does direct marketing reach us?

1 Through the mail

A 'classic mailshot' usually contains four elements: a letter introducing the package; an explanatory brochure of some sort; and a reply device; all packaged in an outer envelope.

2 Loose inserts

One-piece direct marketing vehicles are frequently included in magazines, journals, newspapers and in other people's mailings. The actual format may vary – flyer, L-shaped card, self-mailer, and so on – but it must include all the basic elements of the mailshot.

3 Off-the-page advertising

The reply device is usually either a coupon or a telephone number so that the reader can order 'off the page'.

4 Catalogues

Anything from a substantial bound book with a huge variety of products to a simple brochure containing a specific range of goods (e.g. maternity clothes or bulbs for the garden).

5 Card deck mailings

A collection of cards usually mailed in a plastic envelope, with a covering letter, to individuals at work. Each card features details of a product on one side and ordering details on the other and is returned direct to the mailer for fulfilment. Individuals pass on cards they know will interest their colleagues.

6 Party plan selling

Most people have heard of Tupperware (TM) parties but today a wide variety of goods are sold at home, from books and costume jewellery to fine wine and paintings. The refreshments on offer, and the knowledge that the hostess gets a commission on sales, usually add a degree of pressure to the selling.

7 Door-to-door

The Jehovah's Witnesses solicit on this basis, as do double-glazing salespeople. The most important factor is choosing the right area for the kind of product you are selling. For instance stick-on stonework to make your house look like a Cotswold cottage is unlikely to go down well in the conservation area of a town.

8 Telemarketing

Selling over the telephone should include inbound calls (handling them properly to ensure that the majority of enquiries are converted into orders) as well as outbound (selling specific products to lists of prospects).

9 Television shopping

Direct ordering following a demonstration on television has been popular in the US for many years. Satellite television channels are now offering the same selling systems in the UK

(QVC's 24-hour shopping channel was launched in 1993). Estimates show that it is likely to take off quickly – Verdict Research (see Useful Addresses) in a report 'Verdict on Home Shopping – August 1994' predict that the TV shopping market will be worth £300 million within five years.

10   Fax and telex

This is a difficult area, as the company/person you are contacting is paying to receive your advertising material (a) through the cost of paper and (b) by having their machine tied up with your incoming call. Hostility towards the sender can be the result. Both methods are illegal in some US states already, and legislation looks possible in the UK.

Nevertheless, for an established trading relationship, and when there is a particular short-term sales proposition on offer, both telex and fax can work well. For example, fax would be a good method of advertising last-minute places on a training course to companies who had previously enquired about them. A faxed promotion piece, by its very nature, looks urgent.

11   Clubs

Lots of direct marketing sales operations operate as clubs. Some have rules, such as the 'negative option' run by several book clubs (reply by a certain day or receive the book of the month); others merely benefit from a 'club feel' ('buy our merchandise and belong').

Clubs may provide the market with both a convenient way to buy as well as the chance to learn more about a particular interest or hobby. For example, *The Curry Club* regularly offers its members the chance to try out a new dish, supplying both the recipe and all the spices needed. Wine clubs similarly make it easy for their members to try new wines, extend their knowledge and encourage them to make further purchases.

The advantages of putting together a club can be even

more significant when it is designed to cater for a market that is geographically widespread (i.e. very expensive for a rep to cover) or badly served by retail outlets. For example, the direct marketing firm, Wyvern Crest, established a database of horse owners in Britain, with a view to selling goods direct to them at home. As it takes a fair bit of land to house a horse, the list consisted of widely spread names and addresses of people with a keen buying interest in highly targeted goods, and with money to spend. This was an ideal basis for a direct marketing operation. Such an organisation offering to reach a specific market in a new and improved way could ask for very high trade discounts from suppliers whose merchandise it was planning to sell.

12   Promotions

The coupon on the back of the cereal carton asking for your name and address in return for a promotional offer or a money-off coupon may be part of a plan to solicit further business from you direct in future. The same goes for many market research campaigns run by manufacturers.

13   Competitions

If you are sufficiently interested in a company's main product to try and win one in a competition they are organising, then you may also be interested in buying one. For this reason it is very likely that a special purchase offer, targeted at those who were not lucky enough to win the competition, will produce extra business for the organiser.

Although all the above examples are forms of direct marketing, I have concentrated in this chapter on material received through the post, which is much the largest sector of direct marketing. All the same principles apply, whatever direct marketing method you are using.

Who uses direct marketing?

Of the top 3,000 advertisers in Britain, over two-thirds have a specific direct marketing responsibility in-house, and spending decisions in this area are taken at a very high level. For example, direct mail is sent out by a wide variety of organisations, as the following analysis of the senders of consumer mail reveals. For comparison, I have listed the figures for 1988. Note that the share of mail from mail-order companies has gone down, but the amount of mail from other organisations (e.g. charities and manufacturers) is well up.

	1994 %	1988 %
General mail order (e.g. catalogues)	17.9	26.7
Insurance companies	10.2	7.0
Credit cards	4.6	7.0
Banks	8.2	7.9
Building societies	2.5	3.3
Retailers	7.9	6.9
Magazines	2.6	5.2
Travel agencies	*	5.0
Estate agents	0.6	3.5
Manufacturers	6.5	4.6
Book clubs	4.0	4.1
Charities	7.2	3.9
Gas/Electricity Board	3.2	1.6
Entertainment	*	1.3
Film companies	0.7	0.9
Others	23.9	10.2
Total	100.0	100.0

* included in 'other' in 1994

Source: Royal Mail

The myths that surround direct marketing

'No one reads it'

People claim not to respond because they don't like to be thought predictable. The Royal Mail obviously has a vested interest in showing that direct marketing works and so they sponsor the Mail Monitor Panel, a large group of ordinary consumers who report on what they do with their mail. Despite a rise in direct marketing materials received over the past few years, the fate of the mail received has been fairly consistent: four-fifths of it gets opened. For the last item of direct marketing material received:

- 83 per cent had opened it
- 68 per cent of the sample had read it
- And 31 per cent had passed it on to someone else to read

In business-to-business mailings the figures are even more startling. This has been the fastest-growing area for the direct marketing industry (it has grown by 63 per cent since 1987, consumer mail by 39 per cent), and a recent business survey revealed that 84 per cent of it gets looked at. Of the managers questioned, 43 per cent felt direct mail was very or quite useful, particularly so to non-managerial professionals who don't have time to read the trade press.

The Royal Mail publish several informative leaflets with local and national contact numbers. In particular, look out for *The Royal Mail Guide to Successful Direct Mail*. (See Useful Addresses.)

'Junk mail and loose inserts go straight in the bin'

Use the evidence you see around you. Watch those opening a magazine for the first time on a train – most people look through all the enclosures before they put them to one side, thereby allocating far more time to them than to the space advertising in the same magazine.

'It's random and wasteful'

Receiving two copies of a mailshot can convince the recipient that the sender's marketing pitch is haphazard. Lists supplied on computer disk can be de-duplicated against each other to avoid mailing the same name twice, but list overlap is in fact a sign that marketing selection strategy is spot on. Only 46 per cent of direct mail is targeted at cold prospects; 53 per cent is sent to customers with whom the sender has dealt in the past or has an established relationship.

'2 per cent is the maximum possible response; you will most likely receive less'

The 2 per cent response figure is well known within the direct marketing industry but no one, not even the industry's professional organisation, is sure where this figure came from. Regular mail users are doing better, especially from their existing customers, and this despite an increased volume of direct mail since 1985. Since 1985 the proportion of people who respond to mailshots has remained constant at 8 per cent.

In any case, if your product is sufficiently expensive, a low response rate may not matter. Probably the most famous direct mail sale was that of old London Bridge, which was offered by letter to a specific selection of wealthy people who might want to own it, and also had the space to house it. The one sale to a rich American more than paid for the entire marketing campaign.

Another development is to use direct marketing as one stage in a very sophisticated marketing campaign – for example, an initial call or mailshot is used to 'sell' a brochure, a follow-up call or reply card to request an appointment to display the product, and so on. This works well for products which require a lot of explanation (e.g. investments or insurance).

'This is an industry with no controls – big brother is watching you'

Selling timeshare through direct marketing has given the medium a bad name, and the lack of any obvious policing makes it worse. In fact trading practices and regulations are now more stringent within the direct mail industry than in any other advertising medium. Unfortunately the public often doesn't know about the controls. (Contact the Direct Mail Services Standards Board, listed in Useful Addresses, for further details.)

'Direct marketing is extremely tacky and is a passing phase'

Rubbish. The key trend in retailing in the late 1980s is the pursuit of customer service. In a difficult market firms have to struggle to maintain market share, and many direct marketing operations work because the customer likes to buy that way. Distinctions are blurring – general retailers are now offering certain products (e.g. wine, flowers and life assurance) direct to their retail customers at home; charities are shifting from tin-rattling on Saturday morning to making appeals direct. The direct marketing industry is growing and becoming highly professional, aided by more widely available and cheaper technology.

Why has direct marketing grown so fast?

In difficult trading conditions advertisers demand greater accountability. Direct marketing offers value for money because it is testable; and the industry's figures show that the promotions are getting more specific, thus exploiting the medium's key advantages. If every recipient is chucking all the direct marketing material they receive in the bin then a large industry, employing over 25,000 people, is surviving on nothing.

	Press	TV	Outdoor & Transport	Radio	Cinema	Direct Mail	Total
1988	4507	2127	244	139	27	530	7574
1989	5077	2286	271	159	35	758	8586
1990	5076	2325	282	163	39	979	8864
1991	4816	2313	267	149	42	895	8482
1992	4957	2472	284	157	45	945	8860
1993	5103	2605	300	194	49	904	9155
1994	-	-	-	-	-	1049	-

Advertising expenditure (million pounds)

Source: Advertising Association

Estimated share of total expenditure in 1994

	%
Press	55.3
TV	28.1
Direct Mail	10.3
Outdoor & Transport	3.4
Radio	2.3
Cinema	0.6
Total	100.0

Source: Direct Mail Information Service based on Advertising Association data

Television viewers increasingly regard advertisements as entertainment rather than promotion, and remote control has given them the power to 'zap' at the start of a commercial break. At the same time, traffic congestion in city centres and parking problems have made the high streets inaccessible. Shopping from home by direct marketing offers the customer a number of very significant advantages, not least the chance to choose in peace.

What advantages does direct marketing offer?

Direct marketing is an effective method of selling and it is very cash positive because, at the moment, most direct marketing asks for payment with order. This obviously makes good financial sense and pleases the company accountants! What is more, direct supply means that no retail discount is being given away. Even allowing for the costs of promotion, the economics of direct sales are usually better than those of retail sales. (For the future, however, it should be noted that the EC is in the process of producing a directive on distance selling. This is currently in draft stage, but is expected to be in force by 1996. The *original* draft prohibited cash with order.)

In addition, the direct marketer has more control over the various elements of the marketing mix (discussed in Chapter 1) than with any other means of promotion. With direct marketing you can target a very specific market, holding the prospect's attention, at the time you have chosen. Because you have the recipient's undivided attention for as long as they keep reading, this is the next best thing to an explanatory visit from a rep (even better value for money in geographically inaccessible areas).

Furthermore, you can see very quickly whether a marketing strategy is working – or not. Very few other marketing methods offer such direct feedback, so quickly. And direct marketing is excellent in combination with other marketing methods. Increasingly, direct marketing gets used as one stage in a marketing campaign.

What kind of products sell bes through direct marketing?

Even the cheapest mailshot, allowing for postage, production and despatch costs, will probably cost at least £300 per thousand. It follows that if you try to sell low-priced goods a very high response rate is needed for the promotion to break even. As a rule of thumb I would not try to direct-market a product worth less than £30 or £40.

The alternative is to offer a variety of goods in the hope of getting a bigger order. For example, the Red House Book Club, based in Oxford, run an extremely successful children's party supply service. Prices of goods in the catalogue range from 30p to £6.95, with an incentive for ordering above £15 plus postage and packing. The average order is £18.

Unless you are offering a specific new service benefit, it is probably easier to market new goods to existing or new markets, rather than trying to market existing goods for which established buying patterns exist. For example, I doubt that I would be interested in buying children's shoes through the post, as these buying decisions depend heavily on the personal involvement and training of the fitter. On the other hand, an opportunity to buy the basics of school uniform, deliverable to my door at no additional cost at a time when the shops are crowded, would be most attractive.

It is also important to make sure that you can reach your target market at a reasonable cost. It's no use deciding to market a specific product to a particular market if a list to reach them does not exist and can only be built at a substantial cost.

In any direct marketing campaign, the list of prospective customers to be contacted is what really matters.

It's often true that those responsible for direct marketing worry about the wrong things. Advertising proofs are pored over, in-jokes are delighted in, colours are carefully matched with the art director's samples. But no one ever failed to buy direct because the leaflet was typeset in Times rather than Garamond. This is the wrong way round. Remember the central importance of the customer, and don't take the list of prospective customers for granted. Send the best possible mailshot to the worst possible list and you will fail. On the other hand, the worst possible mailshot sent to the best possible list has a good chance of success.

Where do address lists come from?

Most direct marketing is based on rented lists: a glance through some list-brokers' catalogues will reveal a wide variety (and substantial overlap). The range is wide – anything from purchasers of thermal underwear to subscribers to specific magazines. The cost of renting starts from around £50 per thousand, and may go up to several hundred pounds per thousand for a highly targeted list. There is often a minimum rental quantity (say 5,000 or 10,000), and an additional per thousand charge for any 'selection criteria' you require when the list is produced (e.g. geographical area, household income, age and so on).

To find these list-brokers, I would recommend looking in the trade press – likely magazines are: *Marketing Week*; *Marketing*; *Precision Marketing* and *Direct Response*. If you have specific list requirements, ring the Direct Marketing Association (see Useful Addresses). They can put you in touch with brokers likely to be able to help, all of whom adhere to the DMA's Code of Practice.

Alternatively, lists may be bought outright (from list owners); built yourself (if you think you are likely to need them again); swapped (with manufacturers approaching the same market with a non-competing product); or purloined (association or membership lists, directory entries and so on).

Buy any sort of product through the post and, unless you tick the box saying you do not want any further information sent to you, you are likely to end up on a mailing database, with the details of your specific purchase recorded. The supplier may either re-mail you or rent your name to a third party.

The most useful thing for any potential direct marketer to develop is a list mentality – both for existing and potential list opportunities. For example, if you were thinking of offering a service supplying wine direct to consumers, it is unlikely that any existing wine service would agree to rent you their list. So you would have to apply lateral thinking. What other products might those who love fine wine also buy? Expensive holidays? Subscriptions to *The Economist*? Particular makes of car?

What should you include?

The type of sales message you develop to approach your target market will obviously depend on what you are selling and how. For example, for a telemarketing campaign you need to provide the callers with a list of key benefits to put across, as well as the answers to difficult questions the potential customer is likely to come up with. For a very detailed product being sold to a highly technical audience, you may wish to offer an explanatory brochure backed up by an invitation to a demonstration.

As we have seen, most mailshots consist of four items – an outer envelope (usually with a message on), a letter, a brochure and a reply envelope. Sometimes other elements are added, such as a second order form, an additional letter from a satisfied user and/or a money-off coupon. But the two real essentials in any form of direct marketing are an explanation of the key product benefits and the opportunity to order.

Explain the key product benefits

How to explain and present the key product benefits in direct marketing campaigns could easily fill a chapter on its own. The best advice is to bear in mind that most people reading (or listening to) advertising copy are in a hurry, so there is no time for gentle introductions and explanations of background information. Your copy should make it absolutely clear what the product benefits are, and should be divided up into tempting chunks to encourage the customer to continue reading.

Concentrate on the market's need to know, not your need to tell. Product benefits appeal to the market, product features to you. For example, the wine supply service might feature specially sourced, unusual wines that are bought and imported direct. The benefit to the market is that they do not have to do the searching themselves and they are securing a quality product that not everyone else will have.

Write as if you were writing a letter; make it personal and chatty (without being patronising). Good copy has the quality of a conversation and keeps you reading. To check whether yours reaches the mark, read it aloud. Better still, get someone else to read it aloud. Answer all questions you would want answered if you were standing in a shop listening to a sales assistant before making a decision to buy.

Large-scale direct marketers, with money to spend, experiment with different formats. What they almost never do is omit the letter, as this is the item of the mailing that gets the highest noting. Even within the accompanying letter there are certain key spots – the headline, the signature and the P.S. (apparently because when receiving a letter from an unfamiliar person, we automatically look to the signature block to see who it is from, and then our eyes fall to the P.S.; it follows that a really key selling benefit should be restated here).

Do repeat your key sales messages (although using different words each time). Very few, if any, recipients will read the copy through from start to finish. Allow for their reading habits and make sure you get the key sales benefits across.

The best way to learn how to write good copy is to get on the receiving end of as many examples as possible. The Mailing Preference Service (see Useful Addresses) can help here. Most people write to it to ask to be removed from mailing lists. The direct marketing professionals on their computer files are easily identifiable because they have asked to receive *more*. The charities, in particular, are masters at presenting a sales message through the post. (For further advice on creating easy-to-read copy and design, see Chapter 7.)

Give the customer the opportunity to order (the response vehicle)

Again, it is vital that the response vehicle considers the market, restates the main benefits and makes it really easy to reply.

Think about how the potential customer likes to order. Do they have purchasing power or will the order form be passed to a higher authority for signature? Organise your layout accordingly. Would they find it more convenient to order over the telephone? Would a direct fax line make it even easier? Is your customer service line manned by real people after traditional shop hours? If so, say so. Think about how you react when placing direct orders, and what annoys you.

Anything that makes the recipient delay ordering should be rejected – reply spaces that are too small to write your name and address in, postage and packing arrangements that are not instantly comprehensible, the absence of a reply envelope if the customer is meant to pay by cheque (meaning that the customer has to hunt for one), asking for a credit card number on a reply postcard (would you really give yours?)

How do you get your message to the market?

Most direct marketing materials go out through mailing fulfilment houses (listed in *Yellow Pages*), but a similar service could be provided by your own company's post room.

Talk to your mailing house at an early stage and you will
save money. For example, the first weight band for second-
class post in the UK is 60 grams. Adding another order form
to your mailing or including an insert for someone else is
unlikely to increase your postage costs but may make the
economics of mailing better.

The outer envelope is the first piece of promotional material the market sees, so put a sales message on it. All outer
envelopes need a return address, so you can put a sales
message there at the same time, for no extra cost.

Don't ruin the look of your mailing by using really cheap
envelopes. A prestigious mailshot in a cheap envelope which
allows show-through of colour can look terrible. The same
goes for a thin A4 brochure put in an envelope of the same
size; it will arrive looking battered. You'd probably be better
off paying for a fold and inserting in a smaller (C5) envelope.

The Royal Mail offers a range of discounts on the full rate
of postage to mass mailers. Most large mailings get sent out
through mailing houses who stuff the envelopes and organise
postage. Even if your mailing is too small to secure a
discount, some mailing houses offer consolidation services
or cooperative mailings to particular markets. Ensure you get
the best deal available; if you don't ask about a discount you
may not get offered one.

For a rectangular-shaped brochure, putting the fold on the
short side rather than the long side may mean it has to be
inserted into the envelope by hand rather than done on a
machine. This will increase your costs. Discuss your
proposed format with the mailing house before, rather than
after, production.

Unusually shaped brochures may look attractive, but
finding – or worse still – having to create a matching envelope may cost a fortune, thereby making the whole
promotion uneconomic.

How do you test your campaign?

Most major direct marketers carry out trials before committing themselves to extensive campaigns. Before an important mailing or telemarketing campaign they experiment with small sections of the lists they are thinking of contacting. They try out different orders and different creative formats – to ensure that their future campaigns are as successful as possible.

You can learn from their methods. Look for direct marketing formats that get used repeatedly – a sure sign that they are getting a good response. But when you decide to test your own promotional material don't end up testing so many factors that your results are too difficult to formulate in a meaningful way and so you end up learning nothing.

How do you manage the response?

This can be divided into two stages:

Order fulfilment

This involves getting the orders to the customer as quickly and safely as possible, dealing with any problems or queries, and handling returns.

Data management

The very last thing you should do with the names of those who order from you is to forget them, once you have fulfilled their immediate needs. They provide vital business information; past customers who, provided they were happy with the service you gave them, are likely to buy from you again. (For specific advice on setting up an in-house database, see p. 170.)

Every mailing will produce a certain number of 'gone aways' (often called 'nixies'). Return these to the list owner so they can update their master list. If you receive an unacceptably high percentage of undeliverables (more than 5 per cent of the total number of names you rented), ask for a refund on your list rental and a contribution towards your creative and postage costs.

How do you work out whether the campaign was successful?

One of the key advantages of direct marketing is that it is testable. What is more, you don't have to wait until every last order is back before deciding whether or not the campaign has worked. For most promotions there is a 'half life' stage at which you can predict its overall success.

Monitoring the response can be as simple or as complicated as you like. Running a felt-tip pen down the side of a wedge of leaflets you are placing as loose inserts in a specific magazine will identify which orders resulted from that particular source. At the other extreme, 'scratch coding' a series of identifying marks on your order form will enable you to identify which orders came from which lists, and so to work out your **response rate** and your **cost per order**. (Lots of sales don't necessarily mean you are making lots of profit.)

All this information will of course be very helpful when deciding on the best methods of promotion for future direct marketing campaigns appealing to the same market sector.

How do you work out your profit?

To measure results against costs effectively, you have to calculate the response rate of your mailing:

$$\text{The response rate} = \frac{\text{number of replies}}{\text{number mailed}} \times 100$$

For example, if you have 100 replies from a mailing sent to 3,000 addresses then your response rate is 3.33 per cent. The industry average is often quoted as around 2 per cent, but you should do better if you are mailing to a **warm list** (one that has either bought from you before, or purchased a similar product from a similar vendor).

More important than the response rate is the cost per order (i.e. how much it is costing you to secure each order):

$$\text{Cost per order} = \frac{\text{cost of mailing} \times \text{number mailed}}{\text{number of orders received}}$$

Your costs of mailing will include all the various elements of the campaign: list rental; printing and design costs; copy-writing; despatch and postage. For example, if the mailing of 3,000 is costing you £400 per thousand, then each of the 100 orders will be costing you £12. A quick comparison of your cost per order with the selling price of the product you are promoting will show you whether your mailing is heading for profit or loss.

For more detailed information on how profitable your efforts have been you need to establish the **contribution per sale** for each item sold. To calculate this, as well as the **direct production costs** for the item(s) being promoted, you need to estimate your department's share of the company's **indirect costs** (e.g. staff and photocopying, bad debts and warehousing). In this way you can work out what it is worth to your company to make a sale, and whether or not this really exceeds the cost of reaching the market.

This enables you to calculate the break-even response rate – the response you need to make money. The general formula is:

$$\frac{\text{total costs of promotion} \times 100}{\text{contribution per sale} \times \text{total number mailed}}$$

Alternatively, and more simply, to fix the break-even response rate, establish a production and overhead cost for the item you are selling (say 50 per cent of the sale price of the product) and then work out the following equation:

$$\frac{\text{total cost of mailing}}{\text{cost of production and overhead for product promoted}}$$

Using the existing example, and assuming the product being promoted costs £35 the figures work out as follows:

$$\frac{\text{total cost of mailing} = £1,200}{\text{cost of production and overhead for product} = £17.50}$$

The break-even response rate is 2.29 per cent, i.e. you have to sell at least 68 items. With the 69th sale you start making money.

The equations become more complicated if several different lists are used and rental values vary substantially. (In this case the marketing costs will differ for each list addressed.)

Setting up an in-house marketing database

Once you start getting involved in direct marketing it may seem logical to bring the whole operation in-house; to set up your own mailing lists rather than rely on renting what you need. My advice is don't do it too soon.

Mailing lists go out of date very quickly – we move house or job on average once every five years, more often in some market sectors. It follows that it's often far better to let the people who earn their living from the industry carry the substantial overhead of maintaining the mailing list whilst you get some feel from the market; for what works and what doesn't; or what kind of lists respond best.

For lists of casual enquirers compiled at exhibitions or fairs, if you put off mailing them until you have them neatly housed on a database, you may never get around to it. Instead, get the names quickly typed up on to sticky labels and send them out. (You can get the names typed cheaply by employing someone at home, preferably direct rather than through an agency as they then get a pittance.) Put the *responses* on your computer.

If you do decide to set up an in-house database, you must ensure that it is marketing driven. It must meet the needs of the marketing department first, rather than providing the solutions the software writers find easiest.

This means that any information you are likely to need in the future should be storable. For example, you will probably want to record details of your past business with each customer (e.g. how much they spend and how often they order); personal details (e.g. sex, age and number of people at the same address); professional details (job title, employee responsibility), and so on. You should then be able to select a list from the database on the basis of any of the criteria stored (e.g. all females with more than two children; all line managers working in the south of England).

SUMMARY

Direct marketing is here to stay. It is a sophisticated market- ing medium that offers a high degree of control and value for money. It works best for high-priced items with a defined market for which contact lists exist.

In the future I predict that firms will not use direct

marketing for a series of one-off campaigns but will regard it as an ongoing process. In this way they will sell more goods to a continually expanding market about whom they know more and more.

9

What Marketing Costs

IN MOST COMPANIES you will find that a general view on the value and cost of marketing prevails outside the actual marketing department: that it costs too much and is largely unaccountable. Even those who believe in the efficacy of marketing have their doubts about whether *all* the expenditure is justified. As Lord Leverhulme is said to have commented: 'Half the money I spend on advertising is wasted, the trouble is I don't know which half.'

If marketing is seen as a cost for which the benefits are largely intangible, the behaviour of marketing staff often reinforces this impression. They generally spend more time out of the office than many of their colleagues. And resentment from those who must sit at their desks for most of the day can breed suspicion of their aims, means and methods.

Why, for example, must business with third parties be conducted in (expensive) restaurants? Invoices can wing in from a wide variety of service firms willing to help spend on marketing without promising any quantifiable benefits. The techniques for gaining 'free' publicity discussed in Chapter 4 still cost money in overheads and staff. And even today, with more specialised forms of direct marketing available, it can be very hard to isolate which *specific* marketing activity produced the orders, and therefore which ones to keep/drop next time. With these concerns in mind, this chapter discusses how marketing expenditure should be planned, and how to get value for money.

Drawing up a marketing budget

A budget is a plan of activities expressed in money terms. Managing a budget successfully means delivering, at an acceptable cost, all the promotional strategies detailed in the budget. It is not just a question of carrying out as many promotional activities as you can afford within the prescribed limit. Having a budget allows a company to prioritise about what is and is not important, to plan marketing activities rather than simply respond to promotional opportunities as and when they occur.

A marketing budget should be based on what you want to achieve rather than solely on what you have to spend. For example, it is better to say 'I want to do x, y and z so I need w to spend', rather than 'I won't spend any more than w'. Even if you can't afford to reach a specific market in a conventional way, lateral thinking may lead you to another method. For example, space advertising in a national daily newspaper may be prohibitively expensive, but would the same publication consider running a feature on your product, reaching exactly the same market but in a much cheaper way?

Deciding how much to spend on marketing

The amount you decide to spend promoting a product is usually based on a number of factors, principally:

● your overall objectives (Are you trying to produce an immediate market leader with an enormous splash or launch a 'nursery brand' where marketing is gradually built up to the point of high product growth?)

- your experience of the market (What does it expect/need to get a product noticed?)

- what the competition is doing (Do you want to mimic, be different, or 'make or break'?)

- your production and other direct costs

- your company overheads (storage, staff, sales representation, etc)

- the amount of trade discount to be given

- the product's life cycle (the period over which management will see a return – will it be dead within five years or timeless?)

- any self-imposed constraints on this (e.g. the product must break even by the second year)

- contractual payments/obligations to the producer/developer/author

- whether this product is a springboard for cooperative promotional possibilities which benefit several items or a new manufacturing direction to be launched with panache

Although all these considerations should be taken into account, the amount eventually allocated to the marketing budget (and to other departmental budgets) is usually based on company history. If you propose a total marketing budget that is the same as last year's, it will almost certainly sail through unopposed.

Slightly more scientifically, the marketing budget is often arrived at by taking a percentage of the firm's (or section's) projected turnover for that year: i.e. what you can spend is dictated by what you will be receiving. (It follows, in circular fashion, that what you receive will be influenced or determined by what you spend.) Some companies have tried to improve sales by substantially increasing their level of promotional spending, but if it costs proportionally more to achieve the extra sales that result, the outcome can be financial ruin.

For each new product or service the marketing manager estimates market size and the percentage likely to buy. He or she calculates what it will cost to reach potential buyers and decides where the available resources will have most impact.

Anticipated future income from new products is added to other sources of revenue, such as licensing deals and investment income. Projected turnover for the year ahead, and probably for the next three- or five-year period, is then planned.

Part of the process of establishing a budget is monitoring it afterwards. Expectations are charted against actual performance, usually on a monthly and annual basis. Comparisons are then made with previous years and the long-term plans are updated.

If the overall marketing budget tends to be based on a percentage of anticipated turnover (different amounts being allocated to different products according to need and how easy it is to reach the market), what kind of percentages are we talking about? This is a very difficult area, and the statistics that are available must be heavily qualified.

To start with, assessing overall market size for any specific market sector is particularly difficult: at any one time a profusion of very *different* market estimates may be available for exactly the same product category. Government figures, commercially available retail audit data, trade estimates and surveys of consumer spending can all produce widely varying totals. The amount of advertising expenditure in the same market areas can be estimated by looking at what appears, and working out the corresponding rate card values, but of course these figures do not take into account media discounting (which is widespread) and so the resulting figures are probably overestimates. It should also be noted that the Register-MEAL data shown below only covers TV and press.

Bearing in mind these various caveats, the following figures, kindly provided by the Advertising Association, do make very interesting reading:

Product category	Consumers' Expenditure £m	Register-MEAL Expenditure £'000	Advertising Sales Ratio %
Beverages			
Beer	13,000	124,455	0.94
Vermouth aperitifs	237	6,694	2.82
Coffee	561	33,293	5.93
Tea	714	32,399	4.54
Domestic appliances			
Coffee machines	13	1,054	8.11
Refrigeration	483	2,094	0.43
Food			
Bacon	941	1,634	0.17
Crispbread	44	2,658	6.04
Cereals	780	84,913	10.89
Household equipment			
Curtains	474	391	0.08
Bedroom furniture	514	5,067	0.99
Double glazing	45	9,831	21.85
Household stores			
Air fresheners	67	5,230	7.81
Scourers, detergents and cleansers	131	22,771	17.38
Canned dog food	415	14,429	3.48
Pharmaceuticals			
Cough remedies	77	12,388	16.09
Indigestion remedies	54	12,495	23.14
Laxatives	32	1,229	3.84
Toiletries and cosmetics			
Fragrances:			
female	392	22,670	5.78
male	217	18,467	8.51
Razors and blades (disposable)	121	8,626	7.13
Shampoos	259	13,794	12.28
Shaving soap	54	22	0.04

How the budget is divided up

Three main categories of expenditure exist, in decreasing order of importance.

Core marketing costs

These are the regular marketing activities which are essential to the selling cycle and normally cover all the products and services of the company relevant to the same market. I would include here catalogues, brochures for use by reps, annual reports to investors, and so on. The total sum required for these items is usually deducted from the marketing budget before further allocations are made. These core activities are only cut *in extremis*.

Plans for individual products and services

New products, or perhaps products that have already been launched but need to be actively promoted, should have specific amounts of money allocated for their marketing. The allocation is not always made exactly in proportion to the expected revenue: some markets may be easier to contact than others and need fewer resources. Sometimes older products from the range are promoted on the back of new launches, through cooperative (or 'piggy-back) promotions.

Contingency

Last of all may come a contingency amount to be used at the marketing department's discretion on any individual product or service as good ideas occur. It does not always reach the final budget: during the process of trying to reconcile how much the marketing department would like to spend with how much they have, sacrifices are looked for. The contingency budget is very often lost in the process.

The effect of marketing expenditure on prices

It's a common view that the money spent on advertising gets passed straight on to the consumer, who is therefore assumed to be 'paying through the nose'. This is a gross over-simplification.

Firstly, without initial spending on marketing to launch new products and services, many would never come into existence and the consumer would be denied choice. For a new product, the marketing spend is an integral part of the development costs because it is advertising that persuades the market to buy. Market research on mass market advertising has long shown us this, and the new marketing techniques which solicit a direct response have confirmed it. This is not a slur on our national character but a fact. We are a consumer culture and we lap it up. Nor do we stop reading when we have bought the product in question; advertising then confirms our good judgement.

Secondly, advertising can actually bring about lower prices. In recent years, allowing solicitors and other professional groups to advertise in Britain has had an interesting result: the general lowering of prices as practices compete for business. A similar development has been the launch of cut-price versions of the same service. For example, there now exist chains of conveyancing offices that offer a basic service, staffed by legal technicians rather than solicitors, with individual property buyers doing some of the background work themselves, and all at a lower cost than was traditionally available.

The same goes for heavily promoted branded goods, which attract 'me too' competition. Advertising sets a price standard against which low-price budget brands and supermarket own brands compete, offering the consumer better value and wider choice. For example, offering insurance direct by telephone has resulted in much greater price consciousness in the market, where it was previously assumed that all firms offered roughly the same deal. The same has happened with public utilities opened up to competition (e.g. Mercury versus British Telecom); in such cases advertising the availability of an alternative service has resulted in consumers paying less.

How to afford the money spent on marketing

There are four main ways of doing this:

1   ensuring that you charge enough for your products
2   monitoring expenditure
3   bearing in mind the sensitivities of the market
4   making a profit

1   Ensure that you charge enough for your products

Good marketing carries news of the product to the designated market and persuades them to buy. It does not follow that the market needs to be offered the goods at the lowest possible price.

I touched on the mechanics of establishing the price for a product or service in Chapter 1. Production/quantity equations will tell you the most cost-effective number to produce, bearing in mind the size of the market you are serving; market research will tell you what you can charge for it.

Consumers base *their* buying decisions on a product's value and benefits, or promise, not price alone. A higher price will not necessarily deter customers, particularly if your product has inherent additional benefits, or offers a style benefit (e.g. drinks and cosmetics). In most mature markets, quality becomes the most important consideration, not just price.

As an example of this, Sir Paul Girolami, Chairman of Glaxo ignored the advice of colleagues and advisers to market the new anti-ulcer drug Zantac under licence and price it on a par with the best-selling anti-ulcer drug Tagamet. Instead he priced Zantac at a premium to reflect its superiority, commenting: 'You must not be schizophrenic and say you have a better product and then sell it cheaper' (*Sunday Telegraph*, 13 November 1994). In the event the drug was extremely successful and transformed the Glaxo Group's fortunes in the 1980s.

Once a basic price has been established, it is vital to express it in a way that is attractive and easy to understand (e.g. '£9.99', not '£10.75 plus 15% for postage and packing'). An attractive price pays attention to 'pricing points' (price thresholds above which a product will start to appear expensive and meet price resistance).

For companies offering a range of different versions of similar products (e.g. vacuum cleaners or Christmas crackers), a high pricing point at the top end of the range can make the bottom end look like better value for money and add value to the whole range.

Finally you need to establish your variants to list price – the prices available to those who order large quantities of your product or order regularly (or both). Remember that Pareto's Law says that 80 per cent of your business will come from 20 per cent of your customers, so it's very important to look after your core customer base, whether they are individual purchasers or retail outlets. This means that attention to detail, and making them feel valued, is very important. Setting levels of discount, special prices for multiple orders, promotional incentives for regular buyers – these are all techniques that can turn one-off sales into repeat business.

2   Monitor expenditure

Once the budget has been established, stick to it – or only depart from it in a conscious fashion. In most companies, once invoices have been passed by the people who commissioned the work they are sent to a section of the accounts department that deals with promotion expenditure, where one specific person is entitled to sign the payment cheque. *If you are trying to keep a check on expenditure, this system is the wrong way round.* Instead, you should institute controls at the point at which expenditure is commissioned, not when it is being paid for.

In return for the invoices, the accounts department will probably issue monthly reports on spending levels. Even if you have this service, the figures you receive will be several weeks behind your actual expenditure and I would recommend keeping a record yourself. Probably the best way to do this is to keep a separate ledger on expenditure, one screen (or page) per product or service. Note the budget for that product at the top, keeping a running balance of how much has been spent (or committed but not yet billed) and what still remains. Ask your staff to submit monthly or quarterly expenditure monitoring reports; such a system gives you the information you need instantly.

It may be helpful to decide at the beginning of the year what percentages of the individual product budgets are to be spent on print, design, copy, dispatch and other key elements. That does not mean the proportions cannot be changed. If a mailing list is much cheaper to rent than you expected, can you print more leaflets and use them to reach a further selection of the market, perhaps by putting a loose insert in the conference packs of delegates attending a relevant meeting?

Harness your promotion expenditure to your marketing responses and you start to get very sophisticated market information. If you compare the cost of producing a catalogue with the orders received directly from it (or perhaps received during the period over which it was being actively used for ordering) you can arrive at a figure for orders per page and gain an accurate indication of how profitable your endeavours have been. This is the way the retail trade is run; floor space is compared with resulting revenue and what sells best is stocked (unless specific items are considered part of the service that bring customers into the store e.g. haber-dashery).

3   Bear in mind the sensitivities of the market

A lavish brochure may make the customer conclude that a product is over-priced, bad value for money or stale. On the other hand it may do just the opposite and convince the customer that the stylish product shown in full colour is exactly what they need to impress their neighbours. Only intimate knowledge of the market will tell you which approach is right. Marketing material should be as elaborate and costly as the market needs it to be, depending on the product being sold and the market being approached. Giving all products similar treatment may mean that you are wasting money on some and not spending enough on others.

4   Make a profit

Profit in business is *the* motivating force. Unless you make a profit, the survival of the product, and eventually the company itself, may be threatened. Many firms use a loss leader to attract customers (e.g. music clubs offering cheap CDs), but this is a promotional gambit to gain profitable customers in the long term.

Profit is not the same thing as turnover. You may be trading at a furious pace, with all your production capacity taken up and every item quickly sold, but in fact making no money. As some wag once said: 'Turnover is vanity; profit is sanity; cash is reality.'

Your profit margin is the difference between the cost of production and the price you sell the product for, once the promotion, product research, production and basic company overheads have been paid for. Profit can be used to invest in new enterprises and remunerate shareholders. Long-term and short-term profit aims need to be compatible: will the short-term need to sell, perhaps at a very attractive discount, in order to raise cash, wreck the chances of longer-term, and greater, profitability? (No retail buyer likes to reorder at a higher unit cost than the initial order.)

How marketing services charge clients

Traditionally, advertising agencies took a standard percentage of the price of the advertising space booked as their fee for advice and creativity (at first it was 17.65 per cent, then more usually 15 per cent), then added design and production costs marked up by an agreed additional percentage (usually about the same amount, i.e. 15 per cent) to the total. But media discounts were usually larger than this and there could be squabbling about who actually got the discount – the client or the advertising agency – as well as a fear that advertising was being suggested in publications that offered the largest discounts rather than publications that were really right for the product.

Today there is an increasing demand for precise accountability on commissions earned by agencies. Many marketing services are now fee-based (whether hourly or per project); and sometimes a combination of the two (for example, firms will offer to pay consultants per hour up to an agreed maximum). Sometimes individual payment arrangements are established. For example, one American copywriter gets a royalty on every package sent out using a mailshot written by him; the deal only runs out when the firm find a better package.

Payment periods within the industry are well established. Television advertising time, for instance, must be paid for by the 25th day of the month following the appearance of the commercial; newspaper space by the end of the month following insertion. Agencies do not wish to act as bankers and therefore insist on prompt payment from their clients.

When to Spend Your Marketing Budget

Once a basic sum has been allocated for marketing, the next step is to decide when it should be spent during the year. There are three constraints: when the market wants to be told; when the products are scheduled; and when you have time to market them.

1 When the market wants to be told about new products

Promotion is a seasonal business, and the relative importance of different seasons varies according to the type of product being promoted and the market being approached (e.g. most people buy exercise videos and training equipment after Christmas and try to move house in spring or autumn). It is said that Clive Sinclair's biggest mistake was launching an open-topped vehicle (the C5) in winter; in the summer he might have had a much better chance of success.

2 When the products are scheduled

Timing here is crucial. Promoting ahead of launch can stimulate demand and make the market look forward to your product, but promote *too* far ahead and you may find that interest has both waxed and waned before you can deliver. On the other hand, if you leave promotion too late you may miss the market altogether. Similarly, promotion unsupported by effective production and delivery can lead to dramatic loss in profits. This is particularly true in the fashion and 'craze' markets, such as children's toys. For example, interest in Power Rangers peaked just before Christmas 1994 but supplies were heavily restricted; the result was heavy loss of sales.

In particularly time-sensitive promotions, you may consider having your promotion material packed up and ready for despatch as soon as the timing is best for you. For example, I heard of an extremely successful promotion by a pharmaceutical company for a hay fever drug. The mailshot to GPs was packed up and ready to send out as soon as the pollen count reached its first real high of the year. The result was that just as the first batch of red-eyed, snuffly-nosed patients were coming into the surgeries asking for help, doctors were reading the promotional material on the new drug.

3   When you have time to market them

Plan your marketing activity on a yearly basis so that key events are staggered to keep interest up throughout the calendar. Schedule promotions that are time-related first, then slot in other non-time-sensitive events around them – that way you are less likely to have a nervous breakdown!

How to make your marketing budget go further

Take your budget personally

Think of it as yours and you are more likely to handle it efficiently and carefully. Circulate mailing results; analyse the progress of each promotion; record sales figures before and after promotions; make recommendations on how they could have been better/why they were so good.

Always keep your eye out for marketing opportunities

There may be mailing lists that you could have if you do but ask; lucrative secondary markets may be there for the taking if you only think of targeting them.

Watch what your competitors are doing and how much market share they have. Be interested in your products and who buys them. Develop a general interest in advertising and marketing.

Get better value for money

As with so much in marketing, the quality of your thinking and your ideas is more important than how much you actually spend. A lot of money gets wasted.

- If you are sending your information to standard outlets (such as shops or libraries) use cooperative mailings rather than bearing all the dispatch costs yourself. Surveys have shown that most buyers don't care whether promotional material reaches them on its own or in company; it is the *content* that counts.

    If commercial opportunities for cooperative mailings do not exist already, consider setting up partnerships with non-competing firms to share costs. For example, a firm selling business software might mail with a firm organising training seminars for business people.

    Can you get your products adopted as a promotional incentive? Using the same example, the firm organising training seminars might take stock of the business software sold by the office stationery firm to give 'added value' to each delegate. Can you take exhibition space in partnership too?

- Try different ways of reaching the same market: e.g. through loose inserts; inserts in delegates' packs at conferences; displaying material on exhibition stands. You will probably achieve slightly lower levels of response than through solus mailings but your cost of sales will also be substantially lower. You may be able to reach more people for less money.

- Make as much use as possible of the promotional material you produce. If you prepare a central stock list or standard order form, run on extra copies and use them in mailings, include them in parcels or send them to conferences. What additional uses can you get out of your promotional materials? Think laterally.

● Cut down on the production costs of your promotional material. This may serve the dual purpose of saving you money and also impressing the recipient, who may regard over-elaborate leaflets as being paid for by unnecessarily high prices.

Produce leaflets more cheaply. Save on design bills by producing in-house on a desktop publishing machine. Print on coloured paper (rather than just white) for an attractive effect that is still single colour.

Sometimes you may not need to produce a brochure at all. A sales letter with a coupon for return along the bottom can be a very efficient direct mailshot. (The opposite does not apply by the way; brochures always need a letter to go out with them.) Rather than reprinting the leaflet, update your promotion by sending out a letter accompanied by photocopied pages of reviews or features that have appeared. If you need multiple copies it may be cheaper (and less hassle) to get an instant print firm to supply them, rather than monopolising the office photocopier.

● Use your contacts. Send circulars, with information on your products, to the members of professional societies that you belong to; supply your board of directors with product information sheets to send out with their Christmas cards. Network.

● Cheaply produced leaflets mean that you can change the message regularly. Instead of sophisticated design, concentrate on effective copy and buying reasons that really matter to the market. Remember that unnecessarily complicated design can get in the way of effective communication.

Use free publicity to the maximum

Free publicity does not give you control over the message put over, but it does not produce an invoice either. The pursuit of free publicity should not replace your standard promotional plans; rather it should support them. So, before offering to pay for advertising space do see if the magazine will print a feature for you. Similarly, never offer to pay for a loose insert if you know someone on the editorial board who can perhaps arrange for it to be circulated for nothing.

Negotiate

Always ask for a discount. Everyone selling advertising space seems to understand that no one pays the full rate. Sometimes more discount can be squeezed for sending camera-ready copy (although they won't be expecting anything else) or the fact that it's the first time you have advertised with them. Play for time if you can – the sales representative will probably come back to you with a reduced price. If you go for a series of adverts you should get an additional discount; the same applies if you book a year's requirements in one go.

Do you have someone in the department who has previously had a job in advertising sales? If so, ask him/her to handle space negotiations for you and you will almost certainly lower your expected costs further still. When does the publication go to press? Discuss advertising rates just before, have camera-ready copy to hand, and you may get a very good rate.

Advertising salespeople home in on anyone with money to spend, and before long you will find yourself offered discounted prices, usually at the last minute. It's far better to decide where you want to advertise and then negotiate on price. If you habitually respond to the special offers available from magazines you would not have paid the full price to advertise in, you are on the way to serious overspending. Remember that space costs are only one part of the total outlay (there is also the charge for copy, design and typesetting, not to mention a courier to get it there if you are in a hurry). Try saying 'no' repeatedly to find out just how much can be negotiated off the list price!

Go on a negotiating skills course or read a book on the subject (see Further Reading). The approach suggested is non-confrontational; a search for a win-win solution that leaves both parties feeling satisfied, and happy to work together. If you negotiate a discount so large that it leaves the other party feeling dissatisfied and cheated, will they fulfil their side of the bargain or want to work with you again?

Try to get money in more quickly

- Credit periods tend to vary according to the industry – anything from 30 days up to 90 plus.What doesn't tend to vary is the fact that few companies pay on time. Chase early. Find out who actually signs the cheque – it's not usually the person who commissioned the work in the first place, and is far more likely to be someone in the accounts department. Find out their name and ring them direct.

  Institutions, such as schools, colleges and libraries and most firms, will need an official invoice to pay against (rather than sending cheque with order) but can they be encouraged to pay quickly? State your credit terms on the order form and stick to them.

- As for individual customers buying through the mail or over the telephone, give them every opportunity to pay early, and in the most cost-efficient way for you. Some credit cards charge a higher percentage of the sales invoice than others for the use of their facilities. For example, it is more expensive to accept payment through Diners Club and American Express than through Visa and Access, although obviously the costs must be borne if you think your market holds the former two cards but not the latter.

- Asking individuals for payment with order, rather than the chance to pay later with an invoice, will slightly reduce the volume of orders but improve your cash flow. Can you compensate by offering a lock solid guarantee of satisfaction or their money back? Can you make it easy for them to return the goods if they are dissatisfied (perhaps by enclosing a pre-paid label)? Again, the more you reassure them, the more likely your customers are to order. The

Mail Order Protection Scheme (see Useful Addresses) protects shoppers who respond to advertisements in national newspapers.

- Experiment with special offers. Will the customer's order be larger if you offer a discount? Don't assume that you can't change the wording on your company order forms. Study those you receive from other industries, borrow the best ideas, and experiment with different formats and styles in order to make yours as user-friendly as possible.

- A few years ago factoring of invoices was popular. A firm sent copies of all its invoices to a factorer who paid them (less an agreed percentage for his trouble) and then sought payment from the debtor. The trouble was that one small query on the account from the debtor could delay payment. Meanwhile the factorer, not interested in such details, could be steaming ahead to a court appearance. The message is that it's vital to sort out any small problems that may delay payment straight away.

Apply for all the free help available

Does your firm belong to any professional associations? What could you learn from them? For example, the Direct Marketing Association UK (see Useful Addresses) is joined by many mail order companies but not all marketing department staff regularly attend meetings. Find out about the special interest groups that are part of your trade organisation and get copies of the reports they produce. This is all useful market information that you have probably already paid for through your annual subscription.

How to save money on marketing

When cash crises occur – whether suddenly, due to loss of orders (e.g. a client switching loyalty); or long-term, due to the effects of a recession – firms usually react by cutting their expenditure. The biggest saving is always made by shedding members of staff, but this is very painful for all concerned and tends to be used only as a last resort. For a company looking to save money, it's far easier to start by cutting the marketing budget.

If sceptical eyes are being cast in your direction, you need to combat the bad times with information. You have to find out why some products are selling badly and show that you are making changes to market them more effectively. Compare current sales patterns with those for the same period last year. Are any market changes responsible for the differences? If you are selling through direct mail, did any single list perform badly? Which ones did well? By re-mailing to a new selection of even more tightly targeted names you may still be able to remedy the situation (although the gross margin will still be reduced by having to mail twice to achieve your basic orders).

Telesales can tell you a great deal. Unlike a mailshot, where more than 95 per cent of your marketing effort will tell you nothing, in telemarketing every call yields some information. Talk to the reps and customer services staff. Are products being returned because they do not meet customers' expectations? Is the offer unconvincing? If so, try another.

If cuts are the only option, the key skill is knowing which elements to axe from a marketing campaign whilst doing the least possible damage to sales. The very last elements you should cut are the regular tools of the trade: the advance information, product leaflets and catalogues on which so much of the selling cycle depends.

SUMMARY

Marketing is a precise activity; the planning of marketing expenditure should also be precise. If you plan what you are trying to achieve and chart the results against expectations, you will start to build up sophisticated market information to guide you towards future success.

Conclusion

The world is getting smaller. It is now possible to catch AIDS from any sector of society, in any part of the globe. A recent outbreak of plague in India had repercussions for international transportation that reached far beyond the local area. Telecommunications put us in touch internationally on a scale that former generations would find incredible. Advertisers respond to this by searching for slogans and messages that can be used worldwide, for markets that are actually far more similar than their apparent cultural differences once made us think.

Change is the fundamental characteristic of any market. What is new today is the speed at which things change. What is 'hot' today is old hat tomorrow. Crazes become million-dollar industries – or million-dollar losses – enormously quickly, and their scale can mean huge profits (or losses). For example, Sonic 2, the Sega computer game, took £75 million ($115 million) in its first week of sale.

At the same time, new market areas are opening up, assisted by better communications and technology; and improved logistics are supporting the expanding edifice of international trade. Areas once considered out of bounds due to traditional trading relationships (e.g. former colonies) or political regimes (e.g. the former Communist Bloc) are suddenly opening up to new competition.

Our traditional system of values is changing too. The cult of the 'personality' in the media, and the huge amounts paid for personal revelations, have accelerated a growing belief that an individual's basic loyalty is to his or her own interests, not to any wider grouping. Traditional allegiances, however defined, are less important; today loyalty stands for less. The old morality of debt has gone too. Businesses close down and reopen under new trading names all the time, shedding their previous liabilities in the process.

But the cult of the 'personality' however pervasive, is not durable; hence a tendency in public life for celebrities to back lots of horses at the same time. Media or sports stars known in one field cannot rely on their fame lasting for ever, or even for long enough to amass a personal fortune. So they try to build a reputation in other fields too, to increase cash inflow. In the words of John Lyttle, writing in the *Spectator*, they seek to become 'multi-"talents" to go with today's multi-media: to broaden their shelf life in the pop culture supermarket.'

This explains why model Naomi Campbell and actresses Britt Eckland and Joan Collins start writing novels or making records. These options are interesting to backers and the media because their names are already well known to the public. Likewise pop stars whose 'scream-by date' (a term coined by Marcus Berkmann in the *Spectator*) looks to be approaching start changing the way they look.

But it is not just the famous who are demanding more; we all are. Our expectations are becoming more and more specific; the more we are offered, the more we want. We are getting increasingly fickle. For example, customer service programmes which try to fulfil our every need thereby raise the stakes for every other would-be competitor who wants to join the market. We no longer just absorb information; we expect to take part too. Television is the most obvious example. Younger generations now see a screen as something to interact with, rather than simply sit in front of. Wider channel selection, interactive video and satellite have transformed both the opportunities open to us and our expectations. We now have on-line, real-time, on-screen, intelligent-access – to whatever information we need.

Old habits, once considered part of the fabric of life, are disappearing fast. Home banking and shopping are making inroads into high street profits; computer networks mean leisure time need not be spent driving to an appropriate venue – we can enjoy it 'on screen' instead.

How does one make sense of these huge changes, whether as an individual or as part of an organisation? For any business operating today there is a kaleidoscope of different factors to be considered. How do you decide which direction to take, when and how?

I believe the key requirement for charting your way through this mass of conflicting factors is *an understanding of marketing*. A clear grasp of what marketing means and what it encompasses (more or less everything) helps you to identify what is important. And ability to coordinate marketing strategies allows you to decide what to do next.

It is most unlikely that you will be able to control events, but marketing helps you to respond quickly, and to the maximum possible advantage. Market research can help clarify the possibilities, enabling you to distinguish true trends from passing phases.

Marketing analysis can be as flexible as the shifting markets it seeks to study, because it does not rely on any preconceived ideas. An understanding of marketing shows us how to adapt the product, the message and the promotion to the particular market, wherever it is, guided by precise information on the prevailing political and economic conditions and how they are likely to develop in the future.

The same principles that apply in business are relevant in our private lives. There is a growing understanding that conditions are changing all the time and that we have to be more flexible; we need to keep redefining ourselves and persuade potential employers that skills *are* transferable. No longer can the new recruit to any company assume that this organisation, however big, will provide their pay packet for life. A career projection mapped out one year may be irrelevant in five years time, let alone twenty, as political environments change and takeovers occur. Even in Japan, home of the tradition of loyalty to the company, changing jobs is no longer seen as an admission of career failure. Throughout the world higher education establishments have witnessed an increasing demand for vocational courses, which students conclude are more likely to lead to a job afterwards. Publishers and trainers are constantly producing guides to help us present ourselves better to potential employees.

So that is marketing – a panacea for the challenges of the future. Armed with an understanding of marketing, we can chart our way through a vast array of conflicting factors. We can also begin to understand that, for the future, the only certainty is change, and start to make a considered and appropriate response.

Glossary

above and below the line The traditional distinction between different sorts of advertising. 'Above the line' is paid for (e.g. space advertisements taken in newspapers). 'Below the line' is advertising space for which there is no invoice; it is normally negotiated in a mutually beneficial arrangement between two or more organisations. The usual result is an augmented offer to the consumer (more than just the product being sold), often with a time limit. For example, there are 'below the line' promotions on the backs of cereal packets where coupons have to be collected over several purchases to receive a promotional item produced by someone other than the cereal manufacturer. Today the distinctions between 'above' and 'below the line' advertising are blurring as techniques get used in combination and some marketing agencies offer 'through the line' services.

advertorial Advertising copy that masquerades as an editorial item.

artwork Typesetting and illustrations pasted on to board to form artwork which can then be photographed to make printing plates.

bar code A machine-readable unique product code. The bar code appears on the product package and is used for stock control and sales.

b/w Abbreviation for black and white.

blad A sample of a forthcoming (usually printed) product, often also containing marketing information. Originally a blad meant a section of a book printed early to help in the promotion, and to be shown as a sample.

bleed Printed matter that extends over the trimmed edge of the paper; it 'bleeds' off the edge.

blurb A short sales message for use on product packaging or in advertising material.

body copy 1. The bulk of the advertising text, usually following the headline. 2. Also used by designers to denote the fake copy in Latin used to simulate type in finished visuals.

bottom line Financial slang referring to the figure at the foot of a balance sheet indicating net profit or loss. Has come to mean overall profitability (e.g. 'How does that affect the bottom line?').

brand A product (or service) with a set of distinct characteristics that make it different from other products on the market. Companies attempt to 'brand' their goods in the market place so that their customers receive a consistent image of the product and understand both its benefits and what makes it different from other items on the market. The brand may be the manufacturing company's name, or the product name, or both in combination. The **brand leader** in any market is the best-selling product.

break-even The number you have to sell in order to cover your costs (production, promotion and overheads) and thus start making a profit. The break-even point in a mailing is the point at which enough copies have been sold to recoup the costs of the promotion.

bromide A type of photographic paper. Producing a bromide is a one-stage photographic process on to sensitised paper or film which is then developed. **PMTs** are routinely produced on bromide paper but other alternatives now include acetate or self-adhesive paper.

budget A plan of activities expressed in monetary terms.

bullet point A heavy dot or other eye-catching feature to attract attention to a short sales point. Bullet points are often used in advertisement copy both to vary pace and to engage the reader's attention:

- good for attracting attention
- uneven sentences and surrounding spaces draw in the reader
- allow you to restate the main selling points without appearing repetitious

buyer The person within a retail or wholesaling firm responsible for selecting and ordering stock from manufacturers. Large shops will have a different buyer for each department. The buyer usually works hand in hand with a merchandiser who decides on the specific quantities of each line chosen by the buyer.

camera-ready copy Frequently abbreviated to CRC. Copy and artwork that are pasted up and ready for photography, reproduction and printing without further alteration.

card deck/business reply card/ cardex mailing A collection of reply cards each offering a separate sales message to which the recipient can respond by filling in and returning the card. Often used for selling to business people.

casting off Estimating how much space typewritten copy will fill when typeset in a particular face, size and measure.

CD-ROM Short for Compact Disk, Read Only Memory. A high density storage device that can be accessed but not altered by those consulting it.

centred type A line or lines of type individually centred on the width of the text below. Type can also be centred on the page width if on a blank title page.

character An individual letter, space, symbol or punctuation mark. A character count is used in **casting off**.

Cheshire labels Mailing lists required on labels are available either on Cheshire or self-adhesive stationery. Cheshire labels are presented as a continuous roll of paper which is cut up and pasted on to envelopes by a Cheshire machine.

closed market Closed markets are created when local selling rights are sold to a particular agent. Retailers in a closed market must obtain stock from the local agent rather than direct from the original manufacturer.

coated paper Paper that has been coated to give it a smoother surface on one or both sides, e.g. art paper.

colour separations The process of separating a full-colour picture into dots of the four printing colours (red, blue, yellow and black), done either with a camera or an electronic scanning machine. The separated films produced may then be used to make printing plates.

competitive advantage An offer made to your customers which is better than your competitors' offers.

competitive differentials What a company is good and bad at; the things that set it apart from its competitors.

controlled circulation A publication circulated free, or mainly free, to individuals within a particular industry, advertising sales paying for circulation and production costs. Much used in medicine and business.

cooperative mailing A mailing to a specialised market containing material from several advertisers who share the costs between them.

copy Words to be typeset, often used of material prepared for advertising or newspaper features.

cut-out An irregular shaped illustration which will require handwork at the **repro** stage of printing.

desktop publishing Producing **camera-ready copy** and **artwork** on computer screen rather than by pasting them down on to board; allows easy experimentation with different layouts and formats; increasingly widespread.

die-cutting A specialised cutting process used when the requirement for a cut is other than a straight line or right angle (i.e. when a guillotine cannot be used). A metal knife held in wood is punched down on to the item to be cut. Many old letterpress machines have been adapted to form die-cutting equipment.

direct costs   Costs attributable to a specific project, as opposed to general overheads or indirect costs (e.g. the production costs for a particular item).

display type   Large type for headlines, usually 14 points or more.

dummy or rough layout   A layout of planned printed work showing the position of all the key elements: headlines, illustrations, bullet points, body copy, and so on.

dumpbin   Container to hold display and stock in retail outlets; usually supplied by the manufacturer, to encourage the retailer to take more stock than might otherwise be the case. Most are made from cardboard, to be assembled in the shop.

duotone   A **halftone** shot printed in two colours. This is a more expensive way of printing a photograph than simply using a single printing colour, but can add depth and quality to the image presented. It is usually black plus a chosen second colour. A similar effect can be produced by using a tint of the second colour behind a black and white halftone.

embargo   A date before which information may not be released; often used on press releases to ensure that one paper does not

scoop the rest. Sometimes ignored by the media to secure just such a competitive advantage.

EPOS   Short for Electronic Point of Sale. Machine-readable code that can be read by a terminal at a shop checkout to establish price and any appropriate discounts (e.g. information recorded on packets stocked in supermarkets in the form of a **bar code**). Stock levels can thus be updated and repeat orders generated automatically.

flush left/justified left   Type set so that the left-hand margin is vertically aligned, the right-hand margin finishing raggedly wherever the last word ends. Flush right (or justified right) is type set so that only the right-hand margin is vertically aligned.

flyer   A cheaply produced leaflet, usually with no more than two colours and no more than one fold. Often used as a handout or additional insert in a mailing.

font   The range of characters for one size and style of type.

'free' marketing   The pursuit of coverage, mostly in the media, without paying for the space or airtime used.

gsm   see **weight of paper**.

half-life   The point at which the eventual outcome of an experiment can be predicted.

halftone An illustration that reproduces the continuous tone of a photograph. This is achieved by screening the image to break it up into dots. Light areas of the resulting illustration have smaller dots and more surrounding white space to simulate the effect of the original. A **squared-up halftone** is an image in the form of a box (any shape), as opposed to a **cut-out** image.

hard copy Copy on printed paper as opposed to copy on disk or other retrieval system (which is **soft copy**).

headline The eye-catching message at the top of an advertisement or leaflet, usually followed by the **body copy**.

house ad An advertisement which appears in one of the advertiser's own publications or promotions.

house style The typographic and linguistic standards of a particular firm (e.g. a standard way of laying out advertisements, standard typefaces that are always used, and standard rules for spelling and the use of capital letters).

indent 1. To leave space at the beginning of a line or paragraph; often used for subheadings or quotes. 2. To order on account; 'to indent for'.

in-house and out-house work Jobs that are carried out using either the staff and resources within the firm or those of external companies or freelances.

insert Paper or card inserted loose in a magazine or brochure; not secured in any way.

justified type Lines of type set so that both left- and right-hand margins are aligned vertically – as in newspaper columns.

lamination A thin matt or gloss film applied to a printed surface; often used for book jackets, glossy brochures or packaging which can expect a lot of use. Varnishing has a similar effect and is becoming less expensive; it also adds less to the bulk than lamination.

landscape A format resembling a horizontal oblong, i.e. wider than it is deep (as opposed to **portrait**).

letterpress A printing process whereby ink is transferred from raised metal type or plates directly on to paper. This is the way all newspapers used to be printed.

line work Illustrations such as drawings that consist of line only, rather than the graduated tones of photographs; the cheapest kind of illustration to reproduce.

listing allowance Paying for a listing allowance allows a manufacturer to alter existing shelf allocations in retail outlets and introduce their new products to the shop's range. Many retailers deny that this goes on.

litho Short for lithographic, printing process based on

sticking only to those parts of the wet plate which are to be printed. Usually ink is transferred (offset) from a printing plate on to an intermediary surface ('blanket') and then on to the paper. This is the way most marketing material is now printed.

logo   Short for logotype. An identifying symbol or trademark.

market segment   A group of consumers with similar needs. Such groups are separable by social grade, demographic, ethnographic, psychographic factors, and so on.

marketing mix   Checklist developed by the Harvard Business School covering all the important areas that good marketing should consider.

marketing objectives   What you want to achieve (what and why?).

marketing strategies   How you set about achieving your **marketing objectives**. (Who, where, when and how?)

measure   The width of text setting, usually measured in pica 'ems' (the letter 'm' is chosen because it's the widest letter for setting).

mission statement   A *raison d'être*; a description of where an organisation wants to go and what it wants to achieve; 'a journey with a purpose'.

negative option   A practice used by mail order clubs (mainly for CDs or books) whereby a particular title is sent unless a member responds to say it is not required. For example, the 'book of the month' is often a negative option.

net   The final price or sum to be paid, no further discount or allowances to be made. For example, **net profit** is the surplus remaining after all costs, direct and indirect, have been deducted, as opposed to **gross profit** which is the total receipts, only allowing for the deduction of direct costs.

nixies   Addresses on a mailing list which are undeliverable by the carrier. If these amount to more than a certain percentage of the total list supplied, a reputable list owner or broker will provide a refund or credit.

on-line   Connected to a telecommunications system. Some information dates so quickly that it is sold principally on-line. A good example are the databases compiled by credit screening companies who analyse company performance with a view to assessing credit risk. Once you have bought a subscription to use such a database on-line, you can call for information as often as you like, paying only for the running costs of the link.

over-run   1. Type matter which does not fit the design and must either be cut, or the letter and word spacing reduced in size, until it fits. 2. Extra copies printed, over and above the quantity ordered from the printer (see **overs**).

overs Short for over-run. The practice of printing a slightly larger quantity than ordered to make up for copies spoilt either during printing or binding. It is commercially acceptable for the printer to allow 5 per cent over or under the quantity ordered unless otherwise specified. You will be charged for the overs.

ozalid A final check before printing, unless a printed proof is requested. An ozalid is a contact paper proof made from the film and usually used as a last-minute check on positioning for more complex jobs.

Pareto's Law Well-known rule of thumb that states that 80 per cent of your business will come from 20 per cent of your customers.

performance data Market research term for what is going on in the market.

pica One pica 'em' equals 12 printer's points.

PMT Short for Photo Mechanical Transfer. The production of a PMT is a two-stage process: the creation of a photosensitive negative which is then developed with a chemically sensitive carrier. The line image produced is subsequently pasted down on to board to form artwork.

point of sale Eye-catching advertising or promotional material at the point at which goods are paid for (e.g. showcards, posters, balloons, single copy holders, dumpbins and counter packs for display by the till).

point system A typographic standard measure based on the pica 'em', e.g. 12 pt.

portrait A format resembling an upright oblong, i.e. taller than it is wide (as opposed to **landscape**).

pos Abbreviation for positive, e.g. pos film.

positioning A combination of **market segmentation**, defining *where* you should compete, and **competitive advantage**, defining *how* you should compete.

pricing points Sensitive points in price setting, above (or beneath) which the customer's reaction to the product or service will be adversely affected. Thus £14.99 sounds cheaper than £15. Similarly, a product costing £23.50 could probably be pushed closer to the pricing point of £25 before it started to sound expensive, but the increased selling price would substantially improve the profit margin on each sale.

print run Number of copies ordered from a printer (see **overs**).

pro forma invoice One that must be settled before goods are dispatched, often used for export orders or where no account exists.

progressive proofs A set of printed proofs showing each colour individually and then in combination.

promotional mix How you transmit your sales message to the target market; consists of a variety of different techniques to communicate your sales message (e.g. pursuing free publicity, producing informational items such as catalogues and taking advertising space).

proof-reading Reading typeset copy for errors.

qualitative market research Tries to establish breadth of feeling towards a particular product or service (e.g. How does the market feel about it?)

quantitative market research Tries to assess how big the actual/potential market is (e.g. How many people are aware of the product? How is the advertising message getting through?)

ragged right See **unjustified type**.

ranged left See **unjustified type**.

recto The right-hand side of a double page spread (odd page numbers); the opposite of a **verso**.

register Trim marks should appear on the edges of the artwork supplied to a printer, should reappear on the plates made, and need to be matched up when printing to ensure that the whole job is in focus or register. If the plates have not been aligned according to the register marks, or the marks have been placed incorrectly, the job is said to be 'out of register'.

remainder To sell off unsold stock at a cheaper price, often to 'remainder shops' e.g. discount book stores.

reply paid envelope A return envelope included in a mailing with the address of the sender on the front, to be used by the recipient to send back his or her order or request for information. The envelope bears a sign that return postage will be paid by the sender; the theory is that this encourages the recipient to reply. The technique can also be used for sending reply postcards. There are various means of achieving this – FREEPOST, Business Reply and so on.

repro Short for reproduction; the conversion of typeset copy and photographs into final film and printing plates.

response device How the order or response comes back to the mailer (e.g. by reply card or **reply paid envelope**).

retouching Adapting artwork or film to make corrections or alter tonal values.

reverse out To print text in white or a pale colour 'reversed out' of a darker background colour, as opposed to the more usual practice of printing in dark ink on a pale background. This technique can be very effective in small doses, but can make lengthy passages of text very hard to read.

roman Upright type, as opposed to *italic*.

rrp Short for recommended retail price. Usually set by the manufacturer, this is the basis for calculating the discount given to the retailer. In most industries the actual selling price is decided by the retailer, who may choose to lower prices and take a reduced profit margin in order to shift a greater quantity.

run of paper Refers to positioning an advertisement in a particular journal or paper wherever there is room, at the editor's or designer's discretion. This is usually cheaper than specifying a particular (or preferred) position.

saddle stitching A method of binding pamphlets or small books (48-64 pages is probably the limit for saddle stitching successfully). Wire staples or thread are used to stitch along the line of the fold. Also called **wire stitching**.

sale or return Goods supplied to retail outlets on the basis that if they do not sell within a specified period, they may be returned to the producer, the retailer paying only for what has been sold. This leaves the risk with the producer. The opposite of 'firm sale'.

screen 1. The process used to convert continuous tone photographs into patterns of dots, in order to reproduce the effect of the original when printed (see **halftone**). A coarse screen is used in the preparation of illustrations for newsprint

and other less demanding jobs. 2. Short for silk screen printing.

self-mailer A direct mail piece without an envelope or separate outer wrapping. Often used to refer to all-in-one leaflets which combine the sales message and the response device. Space for copy is limited and so this format works best when the recipient already knows of the product being advertised.

serif; sans serif A serif typeface has 'handles' on the letters; sans serif is the opposite.

showthrough How much ink on one side of a printed sheet of paper can be seen on the other side.

shrinkage Disappearance of goods without payment, usually through theft.

solus mailing A mailing to a specialised market containing material from only one advertiser.

specs 1. Short for type specifications. Designers talk about 'doing the spec' by which they mean laying down the parameters of text design – choosing a typeface and size. 2. The specifications for printing a job are all the production details (format, extent, illustrations, **print run**, etc) sent to printers for a quote.

SWOT analysis A useful formula to help you examine your internal Strengths and Weaknesses and your external Opportunities and Threats.

targeting Reaching the right person or market.

telemarketing/teleselling Using the telephone to sell.

terms The discount and credit conditions on which a manufacturer supplies stock to a retailer or wholesaler. Terms will vary according to the amount of stock taken and whether it is accepted **firm** or on a **sale or return** basis.

tint A pattern of printed dots that reproduces as a tone. Using tints is a good way to get value from your printing inks. For example, even if you only have one printing colour, try putting the text in solid, and using a 10 per cent tint of the same colour to fill in and highlight certain boxes around copy. Further variations can be achieved if you are using more printed colours.

trade discount The discount given by manufacturers to retailers or wholesalers on the recommended retail price at which they will subsequently sell the goods. The amount of discount given usually varies according to the amount of stock taken or the amount of promotion promised. 'Short discounts' are small discounts.

trim Short for trimmed size of a printed piece of paper, i.e. its final or guillotined size.

turnover Total invoice value over a specified period for a particular company, including both purchases and sales.

type area The area on the final page that will be occupied by type and illustrations, allowing for the blank border that normally surrounds text.

typeface The style of type, e.g. Garamond or Helvetica. Most typesetting agencies offer posters or leaflets showing all the typefaces they have available, and can obtain additional ones on your behalf.

typescript The **hard copy** (usually typed or a print out) of the manuscript or copy to be reproduced and printed.

typo Short for typographical error; a mistake in the setting introduced by the typesetter.

unjustified type Lines of type set so that the right hand margin does not align vertically and thus appears ragged. This can also be described as 'ranged left' or 'ragged right'.

upper and lower case Upper case characters are CAPITALS, as opposed to lower case.

verso The left-hand side of a double page spread (even page numbers); the opposite of a **recto**.

weight of paper Paper is sold in varying weights defined in gsm or g/m2 (grams per square metre). Printers can offer you samples of various papers in different weights.

white goods Consumer durables

for the kitchen: fridges, cookers and so on.

wholesaler A company that buys products in bulk from manufacturers in order to supply retail outlets and other organisations; often requiring higher than usual discounts in return for the large quantities taken.

wire stitching See **saddle stitching**.

Useful Addresses

MARKETING

The Chartered Institute of Marketing
Moor Hall
Cookham
Maidenhead
Berkshire SL6 9QH
Tel: 01628 427500
Fax: 01628 427499
Europe's largest professional body for marketing and sales practitioners (24,500 members and over 35,000 registered students worldwide). Concerned with maintaining high standards in the industry and promoting a customer-driven, marketing-led culture within organisations. Places considerable emphasis on marketing and sales training.

Marketing Week
Centaur Communications
50 Poland Street
London W1V 4AX
Tel: 0171 439 4222
A weekly magazine which reports on news and events within the marketing industry.

MARKET RESEARCH

Association of Users of Research Agencies (AURA)
Philip Talmage
Honorary Secretary
Commercial Union Assurance
69 Park Lane
London CR9 1BG
Tel: 0171 283 7500

The Market Research Society
15 Northburgh Street
London EC1V 0AH
Tel: 0171 490 4911
Fax: 0171 490 0608
The Orgs Book (organisations and individuals providing market research services) is produced annually. Available free of charge but send £2 to cover postage and packing.

Verdict Research Ltd
112 High Holborn
London WC1V 6JS
Tel: 0171 404 5042
Fax: 0171 430 0059

ADVERTISING

The Advertising Association
Abford House
15 Wilton Road
London SW1V 1NJ
Tel: 0171 828 2771
Fax: 0171 931 0376

A federation of trade associations and professional bodies representing advertisers, agencies, the media and support services; this is the only organisation that speaks for all sides of an industry worth £9 billion in 1994. On behalf of its members, the Association aims to secure and uphold the freedom to advertise as an integral part of the freedom of expression; to explain how advertising works and to promote and maintain high standards in the industry.

Advertising Standards Authority (ASA) and Committee of Advertising Practice (CAP)
Brook House
2-6 Torrington Place
London WC1E 7HN
Tel: 0171 580 5555
Fax: 0171 631 3051
The people you complain to about non-broadcast advertisements you don't consider legal, decent, honest and truthful. The ASA has produced the British Code of Advertising Practice.

Broadcast Advertising Clearance Centre (BACC)
ITV Network Centre
200 Grays Inn Road
London WC1X 8HF
Tel: 0171 843 8265
Fax: 0171 843 8154
Launched in June 1993, this is a replacement for the former ITV Association's copy clearance unit for radio and television commercials. In addition to its former

responsibilities, the new organisation covers all the additional commercial opportunities now open to broadcast advertisers, for example SKY TV, GMTV, Channel Four, S4C and UK Gold as well as all the radio stations in the Association of Independent Radio Companies. The organisation sets standards, enforces compliance and considers all complaints.

The Communication, Advertising and Marketing Education Foundation Ltd (CAM Foundation)
Abford House
15 Wilton Road
London SW1V 1NJ
Tel: 0171 828 7506
Fax: 0171 976 5140
The organisation that administers the marketing industry's professional examinations. For information on the syllabuses, examinations, entry requirements and course details, please contact this address.

Incorporated Society of British Advertisers (ISBA)
44 Hertford Street
London W1Y 8AE
Tel: 0171 499 7502
Fax: 0171 629 5355
A representative organisation for those advertising – over 1,000 companies in the UK belong. Can provide professional advice on areas of potential difficulty, e.g. production costs, formulation of agency/supplier agreements, methods of paying

suppliers, agency evaluation systems, and so on.

Institute for Practitioners in Advertising (IPA)
44 Belgrave Square
London SW1X 8QS
Tel: 0171 235 7020
Fax: 0171 245 9904
The professional organisation for UK advertising agencies concerned with the creating and/or placing of advertising.

MANAGEMENT CONSULTANCY

The Institute of Management
Management House
Cottingham Road
Corby
Northants NN17 1TT
Tel: 01536 204222
Fax: 01536 201651

Institute of Management Consultants
5th Floor
32-33 Hatton Garden
London EC1N 8DL
Tel: 0171 242 2140
Fax: 0171 831 4597
The institute for professional and qualified management consultants in the UK and Republic of Ireland. Includes 3,400 individual members and 300 registered practices. Members are admitted and certified on the basis of an independent assessment of their competence and experience, and agree to abide by the Institute's Code of Professional Conduct.

The Institute runs a Client Support Service which can provide a shortlist of candidates for specific projects.

PUBLIC RELATIONS

Institute of Public Relations (IPR)
Old Trading House
15 Northburgh Street
London EC1V 0PR
Tel: 0171 253 5151
Fax: 0171 490 0588
Has over 5,000 members and is the only UK organisation representing the interests of individual public relations practitioners.

PR Week
Haymarket Business Publications
22 Lancaster Gate
London W2 3LP
Tel: 0181 943 5000
A weekly magazine which reports on news and events within the PR industry.

Public Relations Consultants Association Ltd (PRCA)
Willow House
Willow Place
London SW1P 1JH
Tel: 0171 233 6026
Fax: 0171 828 4797
Looks after the interests of the larger PR firms and offers an information service for potential clients.

SALES PROMOTION

The Institute of Sales Promotion

Arena House
66-68 Pentonville Road
London N1 9HS
Tel: 0171 837 5340
Fax: 0171 837 5326

A very broad representative organisation that looks after the interests of all involved in the sales promotion industry: client companies, agencies and suppliers. Deals particularly with legal issues, runs training courses and makes industry awards. NB: The Advertising Standards Authority (see p. 209) has produced the British Code of Sales Promotion Practice.

Sales Promotion Consultants Association

Arena House
66-68 Pentonville Road
London N1 9HS
Tel: 0171 837 7459
Fax: 0171 278 2930

A trade association that represents the leading UK sales promotion consultancies.

DIRECT MARKETING

Data Protection Registrar's Office

Wycliffe House
Water Lane
Wilmslow
Cheshire SK9 5AX
Tel: 01625 545745
Fax: 01625 524510

All computer-held mailing lists that store personal information have to be registered with the Data Protection Registrar. If you suspect that incorrect information about you is being held on a specific firm's computer files, you can apply to that company to view it (in return for a small fee).

The Direct Mail Information Service

5 Carlisle Street
London W1V 5RG
Tel: 0171 494 0482
Fax: 0171 494 0455

The source of official statistics on direct mail. It also provides the advertising industry, trade and national press with regular reports and updates on research into major trends and relevant issues within the direct mail industry. Run for the Royal Mail by the HBH Partnership, who also offer direct marketing consultancy.

The Direct Mail Services Standards Board (DMSSB)

26 Eccleston Street
London SW1W 9PY
Tel: 0171 824 8651
Fax: 0171 824 8574

An independent and self-regulatory body which aims to maintain the highest standards of practice in direct mail.

The Direct Marketing Association UK Ltd (DMA)

Haymarket House
1 Oxendon Street
London SW1Y 4EE
Tel: 0171 321 2525
Fax: 0171 321 0191

The representative organisation that promotes the interests of the UK's direct marketers.

Mailing Preference Service
Freepost 22
London W1E 7EZ
Contact them if you would like to receive more or less direct mail on a whole range of specific subjects.

Mail Order Protection Scheme
Newspaper Publishers
Association Ltd
16 Took's Court
London EC4A 1LB
Display advertisements in national newspapers that ask for money in advance must conform to this scheme. For full details send a stamped addressed envelope to the above address.

Mail Order Traders Association
100 Old Hall Street
Liverpool L3 9TD
Tel: 0151 227 4181
Fax: 0151 227 2584
A representative organisation for the large UK catalogue mail order companies.

Royal Mail Customer Service Centre
Tel: 01345 740740
This central telephone number covers 9 regional centres and you will be connected to the one nearest you. All calls are charged at local rate.

GETTING MATERIAL PRINTED

Association of Print and Packaging Buyers
Honorary Secretary: Alan Jamieson
c/o West Herts Ventures
10 Ridgeway Road
Redhill
Surrey RH1 6PH
Tel: 01737 780150
Fax: 01737 780160
An association of buyers providing technical advice, help with finding printers and general industry know-how.

British Printing Industries Federation
11 Bedford Row
London WC1R 4DX
Tel: 0171 242 6904
Fax: 0171 405 7784
Membership is by company; benefits include advice on sourcing printers and on specific jobs.

British Promotional Merchandise Association (BPMA)
Suite 12, 4th Floor
Parkway House
Sheen Lane
East Sheen
London SW14 8LS
Tel: 0181 878 0738
Fax: 0181 878 1053

A representative organisation of member companies who produce promotional merchandise. Can help with sourcing suppliers who handle specialised jobs. Produces *Promotions News* six times a year.

Ingram Publishing Ltd
The Lodge
Wardle Old Hall
Wardle
nr Nantwich
Cheshire CW5 6BE
Tel: 01270 528696
Fax: 01270 528604
Publish an extremely useful *Print Price Guide*, giving estimated prices for a tremendous range of different items, on different weight papers and in various colours. Provides you with a basis for judging whether printer's quotations are in the same 'ball park' as might be expected.

OTHER USEFUL ORGANISA-TIONS AND MARKETING SERVICE COMPANIES

Brewer Riddiford (packaging and brand identity)
69 Shelton Street
London WC2 9HE
Tel: 0171 240 9351
Fax: 0171 836 2897

Dragon International Consulting Ltd (naming agency)
Blenheim House
137 Blenheim Crescent
London W11 2EQ
Tel: 0171 229 6090
Fax: 0171 229 4014

The Institute of Logistics
Douglas House
Queen's Square
Corby
Northants NN17 1PL
Tel: 01536 205500
Fax: 01536 400979
The association for professionals who work in the field of logistics. Offers members a variety of services (e.g. legal advice, publications and training) and has a very strong regional organisation.

PIMS (UK) Ltd
PIMS House
Mildmay Avenue
London N1 4RS
Tel: 0171 226 1000
Fax: 0171 704 1360
Keep an up-to-date directory of media contacts which are available in a variety of formats (telephone lists, sticky labels and so on).

The Press Association
292 Vauxhall Bridge Road
London SW1V 1AE
Tel: 0171 963 7000
Fax: 0171 963 7594
An extensive domestic news agency. Send a copy of a press release on a big story to the news

desk and it may end up being circulated to regional papers all over the country.

Reuters
85 Fleet Street
London EC4P 4AJ
Tel: 0171 250 1122
Fax: 0171 542 7921
An international news agency; the London office receives stories for distribution in the UK.

Romeike and Curtice Ltd
Hale House
290-296 Green Lanes
London N13 5TP
Tel: 0181 882 0155
Fax: 0181 882 6716
A cuttings agency who will scan the press for information on/reviews of/likely competition for your products.

Bibliography and Further Reading

Chapter 1: What Marketing Means

Michael J. Baker (ed.), *The Marketing Book*, 2nd edition (Butterworth Heinemann, 1991).
Peter Drucker, *Management, Tasks, Responsibilities, Practices* (Butterworth Heinemann, 1994).
E.J. McCarthy, *Basic Marketing* 11th edition (Richard D Irwin Inc, 1992).
This gives a clear description of E. Jerome McCarthy's system of the 4 'P's for a good marketing mix.
Malcolm H.B. McDonald & Peter Morris, *The Marketing Plan: A pictorial guide for managers* (Butterworth Heinemann, 1987).
This book is presented in a very interesting way; cartoons are used to make sense of complex marketing issues. The book's only drawback is that every manager is assumed to be male.
Colin McIver, *The Marketing Mirage: How to make it a reality* (Mandarin, 1990).
David Ogilvy, *Confessions of an Advertising Man* (Atheneum, 1987).

Chapter 2: Market Research

Robin Birn, *The Effective Use of Market Research*, 2nd edition (Kogan Page, 1992).

Chapter 4: The Promotional Mix

Dale Carnegie, *How to Win Friends and Influence People*, latest edition (Mandarin, 1990).
David Ogilvy, *Ogilvy on Advertising* (Pan, 1983).
An excellent book on advertising, including both theory and practice, now out of print.

Chapter 5: Production and Distribution

Geoffrey Whitehead, *Economics Made Simple*, 13th edition
(Butterworth Heinemann, 1986).

Chapter 6: Employing External Marketing Services

Torin Douglas, with introduction by Barry Day, *The Complete
Guide to Advertising* (Macmillan, 1984).
David Ogilvy, *Confessions of an Advertising Man* (Pan 1987).

Chapter 7: Doing the Work Yourself

Aldous Huxley, *Essays Old and New* (Harper Brothers, 1927 –
now out-of-print).

Chapter 9: What Marketing Costs

Advertising Statistics Yearbook 1994 (Advertising Association,
published annually).

General

Patrick Forsyth, *Marketing on a Tight Budget: A 10-point action
guide* (Piatkus Books, 1995).
Christian H. Godefroy & Dominique Glocheux, *How to Write
Letters That Sell: Winning techniques for achieving sales through direct
mail* (Piatkus Books, 1995).
Vanessa Help, *Negotiating: Everybody wins* (BBC Books, 1992).
Jay Conrad Levinson & Charles Rubin, *Guerrilla Marketing on the
Internet: The complete guide to making money on-line* (Piatkus
Books, 1995).
P. Kotler, *Marketing: An Introduction* (Prentice-Hall, 1994).
P. Kotler, *Marketing Management* (Prentice-Hall, 1994).
P. Kotler, *The Principles of Marketing* (Prentice-Hall, 1993).
Don Peppers & Martha Rogers, *The One-to-One Future: Building
business relationships one customer at a time* (Piatkus Books, 1995).
Stuart Turner, *How to Get Sponsorship* (Kogan Page, 1989).
David Wragg, *Practical Fundraising for Individuals and Small
Groups* (Piatkus Books, 1995).

Index

PIATKUS BUSINESS BOOKS

Piatkus Business Books have been created for people who need expert knowledge readily available in a clear and easy-to-follow format. All the books are written by specialists in their field. They will help you improve your skills quickly and effortlessly in the workplace and on a personal level.

Titles include:

General Management and Business Skills
Be Your Own PR Expert: the complete guide to publicity and public relations   Bill Penn
Complete Conference Organiser's Handbook, The   Robin O'Connor
Complete Time Management System, The   Christian H Godefroy and John Clark
Continuous Quality Improvement   Alasdiar White
Dealing with Difficult People   Roberta Cava
Energy Factor, The: how to motivate your workforce   Art McNeil
How to Choose Stockmarket Winners   Raymond Caley
Influential Manager, The: how to develop a powerful management style   Lee Bryce
Managing for Performance   Alasdair White
Managing Your Team   John Spencer and Adrian Pruss
Perfectly Legal Tax Loopholes   Stephen Courtney
Reinventing Leadership   Warren Bennis and Robert Townsend
Seven Cultures of Capitalism, The: value systems for creating wealth in Britain, the United States, Germany, France, Japan, Sweden and the Netherlands   Charles Hampden-Turner and Fons Trompenaars
Smart Questions for Successful Managers   Dorothy Leeds

Small Business
Financial Know-How for non-Financial Managers   John Spencer and Adrian Pruss
How to Run a Part-Time Business   Barrie Hawkins
Professional Network Marketing   John Bremner
Profit Through the Post; How to set up and run a successful mail order business   Alison Cork

Profit Through the Post; How to set up and run a successful mail order business Alison Cork

Self-Improvement
Brain Power: the 12-week mental training programme Marilyn vos Savant and Leonore Fleischer
Creative Thinking Michael LeBoeuf
NLP (Neuro-Linguistic Programming) – the new art and science of getting what you want Dr Harry Alder
Organise Yourself Ronni Eisenberg with Kate Kelly
Play to Your Strengths Donald O Clifton and Paula Nelson
Quantum Learning: unleash the genius within you Bobbi DePorter with Mike Hernacki
Right Brain Manager, The: how to use the power of your mind to achieve personal and professional success Dr Harry Alder
10-Day MBA, The Steven Silbiger
Three Minute Meditator, The David Harp with Nina Feldman

Sales and Marketing
Complete Conference Organiser's Handbook, The Robin O'Connor
Creating Customers David H Bangs
Enterprise One-to-One Don Peppers and Martha Rogers
Guerrilla Marketing Jay Conrad Levinson
Guerrilla Marketing Excellence Jay Conrad Levinson
Guerrilla Marketing On-Line Attack Jay Conrad Levinson and Charles Rubin
Guerrilla Marketing on the Internet Jay Conrad Levinson and Charles Rubin
How to Succeed in Network Marketing Leonard Hawkins
How to Win a Lot More Business in a Lot Less Time Michael LeBoeuf
How to Win Customers and Keep Them for Life Michael LeBoeuf
Marketing on a Tight Budget Patrick Forsyth
One-to-One Future, The Don Peppers and Martha Rogers
Sales Power: the Silva mind method for sales professionals Jose Silva and Ed Bernd Jr
Winning Edge, The Charles Templeton
Winning New Business: a practical guide to successful sales presentations Dr David Lewis

Presentation and Communication
Better Business Writing Maryann V Piotrowski
Complete Book of Business Etiquette, The Lynne Brennan and David Block
Confident Conversation Dr Lillian Glass
He Says, She Says: closing the communication gap between the sexes Dr Lillian Glass

Networking and Mentoring: a woman's guide   Dr Lily M
Segerman-Peck
Personal Power   Philippa Davies
Powerspeak: the complete guide to public speaking and presentation
Dorothy Leeds
Presenting Yourself: a personal image guide for men   Mary Spillane
Presenting Yourself: a personal image guide for women   Mary Spillane
Say What You Mean and Get What You Want   George R. Walther
Secrets of Successful Interviews   Dorothy Leeds
Total Confidence   Philippa Davies
Your Total Image   Philippa Davies

Careers
How to Find the Perfect Job   Tom Jackson
Perfect CV, The   Tom Jackson
Ten Steps To The Top   Marie Jennings
Which Way Now? – how to plan and develop a successful career
Bridget Wright

**For a free brochure with further information on our complete
range of business titles, please write to:**

**Piatkus Books
Freepost 7 (WD 4505)
London W1E 4EZ**

PIATKUS

GUERRILLA MARKETING
How to make big profits from a small business

(The marketing bestseller, fully revised and expanded)

by Jay Conrad Levinson

Guerilla Marketing simplifies the complexities of marketing to show you exactly how you can turn a small business into a big one and make the maximum amount of money with the minimum amount of investment.

It includes advice on how to:

- Write inexpensive and effective personal letters
- Design small, perfect ads
- Use newspapers creatively
- Organise free seminars and demonstrations
- Use outdoor advertising
- Devise effective competitions
- Employ telephone psychology
- Beat off the competition

Whatever your business, *Guerrilla Marketing* is your indispensable guide to money-making marketing.

Jay Conrad Levinson is the owner of a marketing and consulting firm in the United States. He is the author of several books, including *Guerrilla Marketing Excellence* and *Guerrilla Marketing on the Internet* (Piatkus).

THE ONE-TO-ONE FUTURE
Building business relationships one customer at a time

by Don Peppers and Martha Rogers

The *One-to-One Future* provides a revolutionary alternative to mass-marketing. Rather than selling to as many people as possible, it focuses on selling as many services or products as you can to one customer at a time.

Use Peppers's and Roger's *one-to-one* strategy to:

- find out the 20 per cent – or 2 per cent – of your customers who are the most loyal and offer the biggest opportunities for future profit

- collaborate with each customer, on an individual basis, as you would with your individual suppliers

- cultivate your relationship with each customer by using new, *one-to-one* media – the fax machine, voice mail, touch-tone telephone, cellular phones and (eventually) interactive TV

- develop new marketing ideas to make the most of this new *one-to-one* reality.

Don Peppers is a business development executive in advertising and runs his own consulting firm. Martha Rogers is Associate Professor of Marketing at Bowling Green State University, USA.

About the Author

Alison Baverstock is a leading marketing practitioner and has worked in marketing for nearly twenty years. For the past ten years she has run her own business as a marketing consultant. She has written two other marketing books, ARE BOOKS DIFFERENT? and HOW TO MARKET BOOKS, and runs courses in promotional copywriting and other aspects of marketing.